Getting Started with Greenplum for Big Data Analytics

A hands-on guide on how to execute an analytics project from conceptualization to operationalization using Greenplum

Sunila Gollapudi

PUBLISHING

BIRMINGHAM - MUMBAI

Getting Started with Greenplum for Big Data Analytics

First published: October 2013

Production Reference: 1171013

Published by Packt Publishing Ltd.

Livery Place
35 Livery Street
Birmingham B3 2PB, UK.

ISBN 978-1-78217-704-3

www.packtpub.com

Cover Image by Aniket Sawant (aniket_sawant_photography@hotmail.com)

Credits

Author
Sunila Gollapudi

Reviewers
Brian Feeny

Scott Kahler

Alan Koskelin

Tuomas Nevanranta

Acquisition Editor
Kevin Colaco

Commissioning Editor
Deepika Singh

Technical Editors
Kanhucharan Panda

Vivek Pillai

Project Coordinator
Amey Sawant

Proofreader
Bridget Braund

Indexer
Mariammal Chettiyar

Graphics
Valentina D'silva

Ronak Dhruv

Abhinash Sahu

Production Coordinator
Adonia Jones

Cover Work
Adonia Jones

Foreword

In the last decade, we have seen the impact of exponential advances in technology on the way we work, shop, communicate, and think. At the heart of this change is our ability to collect and gain insights into data; and comments like "Data is the new oil" or "we have a Data Revolution" only amplifies the importance of data in our lives.

Tim Berners-Lee, inventor of the World Wide Web said, "Data is a precious thing and will last longer than the systems themselves." IBM recently stated that people create a staggering 2.5 quintillion bytes of data every day (that's roughly equivalent to over half a billion HD movie downloads). This information is generated from a huge variety of sources including social media posts, digital pictures, videos, retail transactions, and even the GPS tracking functions of mobile phones.

This data explosion has led to the term "Big Data" moving from an Industry buzz word to practically a household term very rapidly. Harnessing "Big Data" to extract insights is not an easy task; the potential rewards for finding these patterns are huge, but it will require technologists and data scientists to work together to solve these problems.

The book written by *Sunila Gollapudi, Getting Started with Greenplum for Big Data Analytics*, has been carefully crafted to address the needs of both the technologists and data scientists.

Sunila starts with providing excellent background to the Big Data problem and why new thinking and skills are required. Along with a dive deep into advanced analytic techniques, she brings out the difference in thinking between the "new" Big Data science and the traditional "Business Intelligence", this is especially useful to help understand and bridge the skill gap.

She moves on to discuss the computing side of the equation-handling scale, complexity of data sets, and rapid response times. The key here is to eliminate the "noise" in data early in the data science life cycle. Here, she talks about how to use one of the industry's leading product platforms like Greenplum to build Big Data solutions with an explanation on the need for a unified platform that can bring essential software components (commercial/open source) together backed by a hardware/appliance.

She then puts the two together to get the desired result—how to get meaning out of Big Data. In the process, she also brings out the capabilities of the R programming language, which is mainly used in the area of statistical computing, graphics, and advanced analytics.

Her easy-to-read practical style of writing with real examples shows her depth of understanding of this subject. The book would be very useful for both data scientists (who need to learn the computing side and technologies to understand) and also for those who aspire to learn data science.

V. Laxmikanth
Managing Director

Broadridge Financial Solutions (India) Private Limited

www.broadridge.com

About the Author

Sunila Gollapudi works as a Technology Architect for Broadridge Financial Solutions Private Limited. She has over 13 years of experience in developing, designing and architecting data-driven solutions with a focus on the banking and financial services domain for around eight years. She drives Big Data and data science practice for Broadridge. Her key roles have been Solutions Architect, Technical leader, Big Data evangelist, and Mentor.

Sunila has a Master's degree in Computer Applications and her passion for mathematics enthused her into data and analytics. She worked on Java, Distributed Architecture, and was a SOA consultant and Integration Specialist before she embarked on her data journey. She is a strong follower of open source technologies and believes in the innovation that open source revolution brings.

She has been a speaker at various conferences and meetups on Java and Big Data. Her current Big Data and data science specialties include Hadoop, Greenplum, R, Weka, MADlib, advanced analytics, machine learning, and data integration tools such as Pentaho and Informatica.

With a unique blend of technology and domain expertise, Sunila has been instrumental in conceptualizing architectural patterns and providing reference architecture for Big Data problems in the financial services domain.

Acknowledgement

It was a pleasure to work with Packt Publishing on this project. Packt has been most accommodating, extremely quick, and responsive to all requests.

I am deeply grateful to Broadridge for providing me the platform to explore and build expertise in Big Data technologies. My greatest gratitude to Laxmikanth V. (Managing Director, Broadridge) and Niladri Ray (Executive Vice President, Broadridge) for all the trust, freedom, and confidence in me.

Thanks to my parents for having relentlessly encouraged me to explore any and every subject that interested me.

Authors usually thank their spouses for their "patience and support" or words to that effect. Unless one has lived through the actual experience, one cannot fully comprehend how true this is. Over the last ten years, Kalyan has endured what must have seemed like a nearly continuous stream of whining punctuated by occasional outbursts of exhilaration and grandiosity—all of which before the background of the self-absorbed attitude of a typical author. His patience and support were unfailing.

Last but not least, my love, my daughter, my angel, Nikita, who has been my continuous drive. Without her being as accommodative as she was, this book wouldn't have been possible.

About the Reviewers

Brian Feeny is a technologist/evangelist working with many Big Data technologies such as analytics, visualization, data mining, machine learning, and statistics. He is a graduate student in Software Engineering at Harvard University, primarily focused on data science, where he gets to work on interesting data problems using some of the latest methods and technology.

Brian works for Presidio Networked Solutions, where he helps businesses with their Big Data challenges and helps them understand how to make best use of their data.

I would like to thank my wife, Scarlett, for her tolerance of my busy schedule. I would like to thank Presidio, my employer, for investing in in our Big Data practice. Lastly, I would like to thank EMC and Pivotal for the excellent training and support they have given Presidio and myself.

Scott Kahler started down the path in the mid 80s when he disconnected the power LED on his Commodore 64. In this fashion he could run his handwritten Dungeons and Dragons' random character generator, and his parents wouldn't complain about the computer being on all night. Since that point of time, Scott Kahler has been involved in technology and data.

His ability to get his hands on truly large datasets happened after the year 2000 failed to end technology as we know it. Scott joined up with a bunch of talented people to launch uclick.com (now gocomics.com) playing a role as a jack-of-all-trades: Programmer, DBA, and System Administrator. It was there that he first dealt with datasets that needed to be distributed to multiple nodes to be parsed and churned on in a relatively quick amount of time. A decade later, he joined Adknowledge and helped implement their Greenplum and Hadoop infrastructures taking roles as their Big Data Architect and managing IT Operations. Scott, now works for Pivotal as a field engineer spreading the gospel of next technology paradigm, scalable distributed storage, and compute.

I would first and foremost like to thank my wife, Kate. She is the primary reason I am able to do what I do. She provides strength when I run into barriers and stability when life is hectic.

Alan Koskelin is a software developer living in the Madison, Wisconsin area. He has worked in many industries including biotech, healthcare, and online retail. The software, he develops, is often data-centric and his personal interests lean towards ecological, environmental, and biological data.

Alan currently works for a nonprofit organization dedicated to improving reading instruction in the primary grades.

Tuomas Nevanranta is a Business Intelligence professional in Helsinki, Finland. He has an M.Sc. in Economics and Business Administration and a B.Sc. in Business Information Technology. He is currently working in a Finnish company called Rongo.

Rongo is a leading Finnish Information Management consultancy company. Rongo helps its customers to manage, refine, and utilize information in their businesses. Rongo creates added value by offering market-leading Business Intelligence solutions containing Big Data solutions, data warehousing, master data management, reporting, and scorecards.

www.PacktPub.com

Support files, eBooks, discount offers and more

You might want to visit www.PacktPub.com for support files and downloads related to your book.

Did you know that Packt offers eBook versions of every book published, with PDF and ePub files available? You can upgrade to the eBook version at www.PacktPub.com and as a print book customer, you are entitled to a discount on the eBook copy. Get in touch with us at service@packtpub.com for more details.

At www.PacktPub.com, you can also read a collection of free technical articles, sign up for a range of free newsletters and receive exclusive discounts and offers on Packt books and eBooks.

http://PacktLib.PacktPub.com

Do you need instant solutions to your IT questions? PacktLib is Packt's online digital book library. Here, you can access, read and search across Packt's entire library of books.

Why Subscribe?

- Fully searchable across every book published by Packt
- Copy and paste, print and bookmark content
- On demand and accessible via web browser

Free Access for Packt account holders

If you have an account with Packt at www.PacktPub.com, you can use this to access PacktLib today and view nine entirely free books. Simply use your login credentials for immediate access.

Instant Updates on New Packt Books

Get notified! Find out when new books are published by following @PacktEnterprise on Twitter, or the *Packt Enterprise* Facebook page.

Table of Contents

Preface

Big Data started off as a technology buzzword rapidly growing into the headline agenda of several corporate strategies across industry verticals. With the amount of structured and unstructured data available to organizations exploding, analysis of these large data sets is increasingly becoming a key basis of competition, productivity growth, and more importantly, product innovation.

Most technology approaches on Big Data appear to come across as linear deployments of new technology stacks on top of their existing databases or data warehouse. Big Data strategy is partly about solving the "computational" challenge that comes with exponentially growing data, and more importantly about "uncovering the patterns" and trends lying hidden in the heaps of data in these large data sets. Also, with changing data storage and processing challenges, existing data warehousing and business intelligence solutions need a face-lift, a requisite for new agile platforms addressing all the aspects of Big Data has become inevitable. From loading/integrating data to presenting analytical visualizations and reports, the new Big Data platforms like Greenplum do it all. Very evidently, we now need to address this opportunity with a combination of "art of data science" and "related tools/technologies".

This book is meant to serve as a practical, hands-on guide to learning and implementing Big Data analytics using Greenplum and other related tools and frameworks like Hadoop, R, MADlib, and Weka. Some key Big Data architectural patterns are covered with detail on few relevant advanced analytics techniques. includes required details to help onboard the readers to all the required concepts, tools, and frameworks to implement a data analytics project.

R, Weka, MADlib, advanced SQL functions, and Windows functions are covered for in-database analytics implementation. Infrastructure and hardware aspects of Greenplum are covered along with some detail on the configurations and tuning.

Overall, from processing structured and unstructured data to presenting the results/ insights to key business stakeholders, this book introduces all the key aspects of the technology and science.

> Greenplum UAP is currently being repositioned by Pivotal. The modules and components are being rebranded to include the "Pivotal" tag and are being packaged under PivotalOne. Few of the VMware products such as GemFire and SQLFire are being included in the Pivotal Solution Suite along with RabbitMQ. Additionally, support/ integration with **Complex Event Processing** (**CEP**) for real-time analytics is added. Hadoop (HD) distribution, now called Pivotal HD, with new framework HAWQ has support for SQL-like querying capabilities for Hadoop data (a framework similar to Impala from open source distribution). However, the current features and capabilities of the Greenplum UAP detailed in this book will still continue to exist.

What this book covers

Chapter 1, Big Data, Analytics, and Data Science Life Cycle, defines and introduces the readers to the core aspects of Big Data and standard analytical techniques. It covers the philosophy of data science with a detailed overview of standard life cycle and steps in business context.

Chapter 2, Greenplum Unified Analytics Platform (UAP), elaborates the architecture and application of Greenplum Unified Analytics Platform (UAP) in Big Data analytics' context. It covers the appliance and the software part of the platform. Greenplum UAP combines the capabilities to process structured and unstructured data with a productivity engine and a social network engine that cans the barriers between the data science teams. Tools and frameworks such as R, Weka, and MADlib that integrate into the platform are elaborated.

Chapter 3, Advanced Analytics – Paradigms, Tools, and Techniques, introduces standard analytic paradigms with a dive deep into some core data mining techniques such as simulations, clustering, data mining, text analytics, decision trees, association rules, linear and logistic regression, and so on. R programming, Weka, and in-database analytics using MADlib are introduced in this chapter.

Chapter 4, Implementing Analytics with Greenplum UAP, covers the implementation aspects of a data science project using Greenplum analytics platform. A detailed guide to loading and unloading structured and unstructured data into Greenplum and HD, along with the approach to integrate Informatica Power Center, R, Hadoop, Weka, and MADlib with Greenplum is covered. A note on Chorus and other Greenplum specific in-database analytic options are detailed.

What you need for this book

As a pre-requisite, this book assumes readers to have basic knowledge of distributed and parallel computing, an understanding of core analytic techniques, and basic exposure to programming.

In this book, readers will see a selective detailing on some implementation aspects of data science project using Greenplum analytics platform (that includes Greenplum Database, HD, in-database analytics utilities such as PL/XXX packages and MADlib), R, and Weka.

Who this book is for

This book is meant for data scientists (or aspiring data scientists) and solution and data architects who are looking for implementing analytic solutions for Big Data using Greenplum integrated analytic platform. This book gives a right mix of detail into technology, tools, framework, and the science part of the analytics.

Conventions

In this book, you will find a number of styles of text that distinguish between different kinds of information. Here are some examples of these styles, and an explanation of their meaning.

Code words in text are shown as follows: "Use `runif` to generate multiple random numbers uniformly between two numbers."

A block of code is set as follows:

```
runif(1, 2, 3)
runif(10, 5.0, 7.5)
```

New terms and **important words** are shown in bold. Words that you see on the screen, in menus or dialog boxes, for example, appear in the text like this: "The following screenshot shows an object browser window in Greenplum's **pgAdminIII**, a client tool to manage database elements".

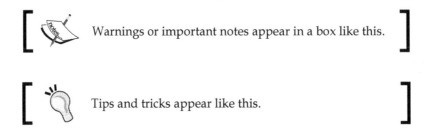

Warnings or important notes appear in a box like this.

Tips and tricks appear like this.

Reader feedback

Feedback from our readers is always welcome. Let us know what you think about this book—what you liked or may have disliked. Reader feedback is important for us to develop titles that you really get the most out of.

To send us general feedback, simply send an e-mail to feedback@packtpub.com, and mention the book title via the subject of your message.

If there is a topic that you have expertise in and you are interested in either writing or contributing to a book, see our author guide on www.packtpub.com/authors.

Customer support

Now that you are the proud owner of a Packt book, we have a number of things to help you to get the most from your purchase.

Errata

Although we have taken every care to ensure the accuracy of our content, mistakes do happen. If you find a mistake in one of our books—maybe a mistake in the text or the code—we would be grateful if you would report this to us. By doing so, you can save other readers from frustration and help us improve subsequent versions of this book. If you find any errata, please report them by visiting http://www.packtpub.com/submit-errata, selecting your book, clicking on the **errata submission form** link, and entering the details of your errata. Once your errata are verified, your submission will be accepted and the errata will be uploaded on our website, or added to any list of existing errata, under the Errata section of that title. Any existing errata can be viewed by selecting your title from http://www.packtpub.com/support.

Piracy

Piracy of copyright material on the Internet is an ongoing problem across all media. At Packt, we take the protection of our copyright and licenses very seriously. If you come across any illegal copies of our works, in any form, on the Internet, please provide us with the location address or website name immediately so that we can pursue a remedy.

Please contact us at copyright@packtpub.com with a link to the suspected pirated material.

We appreciate your help in protecting our authors, and our ability to bring you valuable content.

Questions

You can contact us at questions@packtpub.com if you are having a problem with any aspect of the book, and we will do our best to address it.

1
Big Data, Analytics, and Data Science Life Cycle

Enterprise data has never been of such prominence as in the recent past. One of the dominant challenges of today's major data influx in enterprises is establishing a future-proof strategy focused on deriving meaningful insights tangibly contributing to business growth.

This chapter introduces readers to the core aspects of Big Data, standard analytical techniques, and data science as a practice in business context. In the chapters that follow, these topics are further elaborated with a step-by-step implementation guide to use Greenplum's **Unified Analytics Platform (UAP)**.

The topics covered in this chapter are listed as follows:

- Enterprise data and its characteristics
- Context of Big Data—a definition and the paradigm shift
- Data formats such as structured, semi-structured, and unstructured data
- Data analysis, need, and overview of important analytical techniques (statistical, predictive, mining, and so on)
- The philosophy of data science and its standard life cycle

Enterprise data

Before we take a deep dive into Big Data and analytics, let us understand the important characteristics of enterprise data as a prerequisite.

Enterprise data signifies data in a perspective that is holistic to an enterprise. We are talking about data that is centralized/integrated/federated, using diverse storage strategy, from diverse sources (that are internal and/or external to the enterprise), condensed and cleansed for quality, secure, and definitely scalable.

In short, enterprise data is the data that is seamlessly shared or available for exploration where relevant information is used appropriately to gain competitive advantage for an enterprise.

Data formats and access patterns are diverse which additionally drives some of the need for various platforms. Any new strategic enterprise application development should not assume the persistence requirements to be relational. For example, data that is transactional in nature could be stored in a relational store and twitter feed could be stored in **NoSQL** structure.

This would mean bringing in complexity that introduces learning new interfaces but a benefit worth the performance gain.

It requires that an enterprise has the important data engineering aspects in place to handle enterprise data effectively. The following list covers a few critical data engineering aspects:

- Data architecture and design
- Database administration
- Data governance (that includes data life cycle management, compliance, and security)

Classification

Enterprise data can be classified into the following categories:

- **Transactional data**: It is the data generated to handle day-to-day affairs within an enterprise and reveals a snapshot of ongoing business processing. It is used to control and run fundamental business tasks. This category of data usually refers to a subset of data that is more recent and relevant. This data requires a strong backup strategy and data loss is likely to entail significant monetary impact and legal issues. Transactional data is owned by Enterprise Transactional systems that are the actual source for the data as well. This data is characterized by dynamicity. For example, order entry, new account creation, payments, and so on.

- **Master and Reference data**: Though we see Master data and Reference data categorized under the same bucket, they are different in their own sense. Reference data is all about the data that is usually outside the enterprise and is Standards compliant and usually static in nature. On the other hand, Master data is similar in definition with the only difference that it originates from within the enterprise. Both Master and Reference data are referenced by Transactional data and key to the operation of business. This data is often non-transactional/static in nature and can be stored centralized or duplicated. For example:

  Reference data: country codes, PIN, branch codes, and so on

  Master data: accounts, portfolio managers, departments, and so on

- **Analytical data**: Business data is analyzed and insights derived are presented for decision making; data classified under this category usually is not owned by the analyzing application. Transaction data from various transaction processing systems is fed for analysis. This data is sliced and diced at various levels to help problem solving, planning, and decision-support as it gives multi-dimensional views of various business activities. It is usually larger in volume and historic in nature when compared to transactional data.

In addition to the preceding categories, there are a few other important data classifications. These classifications define the character data:

- **Configuration data**: This classification refers to the data that describes data or defines the way data needs to be used. There can be many categories of configuration data. For example, an application has many clients, and each client needs to refer to a unique set of messaging configurations (let's say a unique queue name) or information regarding how to format a report that needs to be displayed for a particular user, and so on. This classification is also referred to as metadata.

- **Historic data**: It refers to any data that is historic in nature. Typically gives reference to facts at a given point in time. This data requires a robust archival strategy as it is expected to be voluminous. At the same time, it would not undergo any changes and is usually used as a reference for comparison. Corrections/changes to historic data can happen only in the case of errors. Examples can be, security price at a point in time, say January 20, 1996, financial transactions of an account in the first quarter of the year, and so on.

- **Transitional data**: This is one of the most important data classifications that refer to data that is intermediary and temporary in nature. This data is usually generated to improve the data processing speed and could be kept in memory that is evicted post its use. This data might not be available for direct consumption. Example for this data classification can be an intermediary computation data that is stored and is to be used in a bigger scheme of data processing, like market value for each security to compute, and rate of return on the overall value invested.

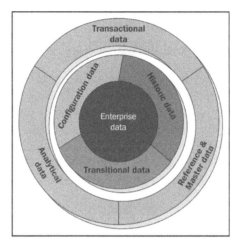

Features

In this section, we will understand the characteristic features of enterprise data. Each of the listed characteristics describes a unique facet/behavior that would be elaborated in the implementation perspective later in the *Data Science life cycle* section in this chapter. Following are a few important characteristics of enterprise data:

- **Included**: Enterprise data is integrated and usually, but not mandatorily, centralized to all applications within an enterprise. Data from various sources and varied formats is either aggregated or federated for this purpose. (Aggregation refers to physically combining data sets into a single structure and location while federation is all about getting a centralized way to access a variety of data sources to get the required data without physically combining/merging the data.)

- **Standards compliance**: Data is represented/presented to the application in context in a format that is either a standard to an enterprise/across enterprises.

- **Secure**: Data is securely accessible through authorization.

- **Scalable**: In a context where data is integrated from various sources, the need to support larger volumes becomes critical, and thus the scalability, both in terms of storage and processing.

- **Condensed/Cleansed/Consistent**: Enterprise data can possibly be condensed and cleansed to ensure data quality against a given set of data standards for an enterprise.

- **Varied sources and formats**: Data is mostly combined from varied sources and can continue to be stored in varied formats for optimized usage.

- **Available**: Enterprise data is always consistent with minimal data disparity and available to all applications using it.

Big Data

One of the important aspects of enterprise data that we learned in the earlier section is the data consolidation and sharing that requires unconstrained collection and access to more data. Every time change is encountered in business, it is captured and recorded as data. This data is usually in a raw form and unless processed cannot be of any value to the business. Innovative analysis tools and software are now available that helps convert this data into valuable information. Many cheap storage options are now available and enterprises are encouraged to store more data and for a long time.

In this section, we will define the core aspects of Big Data, the paradigm shift and attempt to define Big Data.

- A scale of terabytes, petabytes, exabytes, and higher is what the market refers to in terms of volumes. Traditional database engines cannot scale to handle these volumes. The following figure lists the orders of magnitude that represents data volumes:

Multiples of bytes		
SI decimal prefixes		Binary Usage
Name(Symbol)	Value	
Kilobyte(KB)	10^3	2^{10}
Megabyte(MB)	10^6	2^{20}
Gigabyte(GB)	10^9	2^{30}
Terabyte(TB)	10^{12}	2^{40}
Petabyte(PB)	10^{15}	2^{50}
Exabyte(EB)	10^{18}	2^{60}
Zettabyte(ZB)	10^{21}	2^{70}
Yottabyte(YB)	10^{24}	2^{80}

- Data formats generated and consumed may not be structured (for example, relational data that can be normalized). This data is generated by large/ small scientific instruments, social networking sites, and so on. This can be streaming data that is heterogeneous in nature and can be noisy (for example, videos, mails, tweets, and so on). These formats are not supported by any of the traditional datamarts, data store/data mining applications today.

 Noisy data refers to the reduced degree of relevance of data in context. It is the meaningless data that just adds to the need for higher storage space and can adversely affect the result of data analysis. More noise in data could mean more unnecessary/redundant/un-interpretable data.

- Traditionally, business/enterprise data used to be consumed in batches, in specific windows and subject to processing. With the recent innovation in advanced devices and the invasion of interconnect, data is now available in real time and the need for processing insights in real time has become a prime expectation.

- With all the above comes a need for processing efficiency. The processing windows are getting shorter than ever. A simple parallel processing framework like MapReduce has attempted to address this need.

 In Big Data, handling volumes isn't a critical problem to solve; it is the complexity involved in dealing with heterogeneous data that includes a high degree of noise.

So, what is Big Data?

With all that we tried understanding previously; let's now define Big Data.

Big Data can be defined as an environment comprising of tools, processes, and procedures that fosters **discovery** with **data** at its center. This discovery process refers to our ability to derive business value from data and includes collecting, manipulating, analyzing, and managing data.

We are talking about four discrete properties of data that require special tools, processes, and procedures to handle:

- Increased volumes (to the degree of petabytes, and so on)
- Increased availability/accessibility of data (more real time)
- Increased formats (different types of data)
- Increased messiness (noisy)

There is a paradigm shift seen as we now have technology to bring this all together and analyze it.

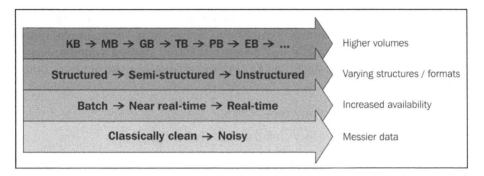

Multi-structured data

In this section, we will discuss various data formats in the context of Big Data. Data is categorized into three main data formats/types:

- **Structured**: Typically, data stored in a relational database can be categorized as structured data. Data that is represented in a strict format is called structured data. Structured data is organized in semantic chunks called entities. These entities are grouped and relations can be defined. Each entity has fixed features called attributes. These attributes have a fixed data type, pre-defined length, constraints, default value definitions, and so on. One important characteristic of structured data is that all entities of the same group have the same attributes, format, length, and follow the same order. Relational database management systems can hold this kind of data.

- **Semi-structured**: For some applications, data is collected in an ad-hoc manner and how this data would be stored or processed is unknown at that stage. Though the data has a structure, it sometimes doesn't comply with a structure that the application is expecting it to be in. Here, different entities can have different structures with no pre-defined structure. This kind of data is defined to be semi-structured. For example, scientific data, bibliographic data, and so on. Graph data structures can hold this kind of data. Some characteristics of semi-structured data are listed as follows:
    - Organized in semantic entities
    - Similar entities are grouped together
    - Entities in the same group may not have the same attributes
    - Order of attributes isn't important
    - There might be optional attributes

° Same attributes might have varying sizes

° Same attributes might be of varying type

- **Unstructured**: Unstructured data refers to the data that has no standard structure and it could mean structure in its isolation. For example, videos, images, documents emails, and so on. File-based storage systems support storing this kind of data. Some key characteristics of unstructured data is listed as follows:

  ° Data can be of any type

  ° Does not have any constraints or follow any rules

  ° It is very unpredictable

  ° Has no specific format or sequence

Data is often a mix of structured, semi-structured, and unstructured data. Unstructured data usually works behind the scenes and eventually converts to structured data.

Here are a few points for us to ponder:

- Data can be manifested in a structured way (for example, storing in a relational format would mean structure), and there are structured ways of expressing unstructured data, for example, text.

- Applications that process data need to understand the structure of data.

- The data that an application produces is usually in a structure that it alone can most efficiently use, and here comes a need for transformation. These transformations are usually complex and the risk of losing data as a part of this process is high.

In the next section that introduces data analytics, we will apply the multi-structured data requirements and take a deep dive on how data of various formats can be processed.

What does it need for a platform to support multi-structured data in a unified way? How native support for each varying structures can be provided, again in a unified way, abstracting end user from the complexity while running analytical processing over the data? The chapters that follow explain how Greenplum UAP can be used to integrate and process data.

Data analytics

To stay ahead of the times and take informed decisions, businesses now require running analytics on data that is moved in on a real-time basis and this data is usually multi-structured, characterized in the previous section. Value is in identifying patterns to make intelligent decisions and in influencing decisions if we could see the behavior patterns.

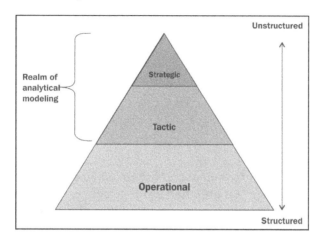

Classically, there are three major levels of management and decision making within an organization: operational, tactical, and strategic. While these levels feed one another, they are essentially distinct:

- **Operational data**: It deals with day-to- day operations. At this level decisions are structured and are usually driven by rules.

- **Tactical data**: It deals with medium-term decisions and is semi-structured. For example, did we meet our branch quota for new loans this week?

- **Strategic data**: It deals with long-term decisions and is more unstructured. For example, should a bank lower its minimum balances to retain more customers and acquire more new customers?

Decision making changes as one goes from level to level.

With increasing need for supporting various aspects of Big Data, as stated previously, existing data warehousing and business intelligence tools are going through transformation.

Big Data is not, of course, just about the rise in the amount of data we have, it is also about the ability we now have to analyze these data sets. It is the development with tools and technologies, including such things as **Distributed Files Systems (DFS)**, which deliver this ability.

High performance continues to be a critical success indicator for user implementations in **Data Warehousing (DW)**, **Business Intelligence (BI)**, **Data Integration (DI)**, and analytics. Advanced analytics includes techniques such as predictive analytics, data mining, statistics, and **Natural Language Processing (NLP)**.

A few important drivers for analytics are listed as follows:

- Need to optimize business operations/processes
- Proactively identify business risks
- Predict new business opportunities
- Compliance to regulations

Big Data analytics is all about application of these advanced analytic techniques to very large, diverse data sets that are often multi-structured in nature. Traditional data warehousing tools do not support the unstructured data sources and the expectations on the processing speeds for Big Data analytics. As a result, a new class of Big Data technology has emerged and is being used in many Big Data analytics environments. There are both open source and commercial offerings in the market for this requirement.

The focus of this book will be Greenplum UAP that includes database (for structured data requirements), HD/Hadoop (for unstructured data requirements), and Chorus (a collaboration platform that can integrate with partner BI, analytics, and visualization tools gluing the communication between the required stakeholders).

The following diagram depicts the evolution of analytics, very clearly, with the increase in data volumes; a linear increase in sophistication of insights is sought.

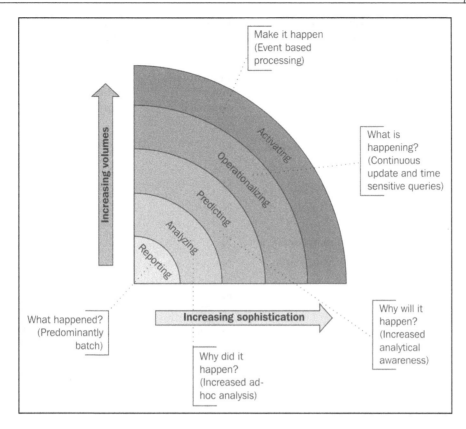

- Initially, it was always **Reporting**. Data was pre-processed and loaded in batches, and an understanding of "what happened?" was gathered.

- Focus slowly shifted on to understanding "why did it happen?". This is with the advent of increased ad-hoc data inclusion.

- At the next level, the focus has shifted to identifying "why will it happen?", a focus more on prediction instead of pure analysis.

- With more ad-hoc data availability, the focus is shifted onto "what is happening?" part of the business.

- Final focus is on "make it happen!" with the advent of real-time event access.

With this paradigm shift, the expectations from a new or modern data warehousing system have changed and the following table lists the expected features:

Challenges	Traditional analytics approach	New analytics approach
Scalability	N	Y
Ingest high volumes of data	N	Y
Data sampling	Y	N
Data variety support	N	Y
Parallel data and query processing	N	Y
Quicker access to information	N	Y
Faster data analysis (higher GB/sec rate)	N	Y
Accuracy in analytical models	N	Y

A few of the analytical techniques we will be further understanding in the following chapters are:

- **Descriptive analytics**: Descriptive analytics provides detail on what has happened, how many, how often, and where. In this technique, new insights are developed using probability analysis, trending, and development of association over data that is classified and categorized.

- **Predictive analytics**: Predictive modeling is used to understand causes and relationships in data in order to predict valuable insights. It provides information on what will happen, what could happen, and what actions can be taken. Patterns are identified in the data using mathematical, statistical, or visualization techniques. These patterns are applied on the new data sets to predict the behavior.

- **Prescriptive analytics:** Prescriptive analytics helps derive a best possible outcome by analyzing the possible outcomes. It includes Descriptive and Predictive analytic techniques to be applied together. Probabilistic and Stochastic methods such as Monte Carlo simulations and Bayesian models to help analyze best course of action based on "what-if" analysis.

Data science

Data analytics discussed in the previous section forms an important step in a data science project. In this section, we will explore the philosophy of data science and the standard life cycle of a data science project.

Data science is all about turning data into products. It is analytics and machine learning put into action to draw inferences and insights out of data. Data science is perceived to be an advanced step to business intelligence that considers all aspects of Big Data.

Data science life cycle

The following diagrams shows the various stages of data science life cycle that includes steps from data availability/loading to deriving and communicating data insights until operationalizing the process.

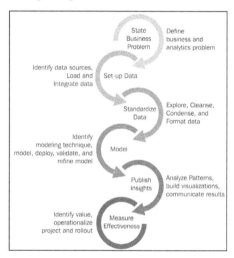

Phase 1 – state business problem

This phase is all about discovering the current problem in hand. The problem statement is analyzed and documented in this phase.

In this phase, we identify the key stakeholders and their interests, key pain points, goals for the project and failure criteria, success criteria, and key risks involved.

Initial hypotheses needs to be formed with the help of domain experts/key stakeholders; this would be the basis against which we would validate the available data. There would be variations of hypotheses that we would need to come up with as an initial step.

There would be a need to do a basic validation for the formed hypotheses and for this we would need to do a preliminary data exploration. We will deal with data exploration and process in the later chapters at length.

Phase 2 – set up data

This phase forms one of the crucial initial steps where we analyze various sources of data, strategy to aggregate/integrate data and scope the kind of data required.

As a part of this initial step, we identify the kind of data we require to solve the problem in context. We would need to consider lifespan of data, volumes, and type of the data. Usually, there would be a need to have access to the raw data, so we would need access to the base data as against the processed/aggregated data. One of the important aspects of this phase is confirming the fact that the data required for this phase is available. A detailed analysis would need to be done to identify how much historic data would need to be extracted for running the tests against the defined initial hypothesis. We would need to consider all the characteristics of Big Data like volumes, varied data formats, data quality, and data influx speed. At the end of this phase, the final data scope would be formed by seeking required validations from domain experts.

Phase 3 – explore/transform data

The previous two phases define the analytic project scope that covers both business and data requirements. Now it's time for data exploration or transformation. It is also referred to as data preparation and of all the phases, this phase is the most iterative and time-consuming one.

During data exploration, it is important to keep in mind that there should be no interference with the ongoing organizational processes.

We start with gathering all kinds of data identified in phase 2 to solve the problem defined in phase 1.This data can be either structured, semi-structured, or unstructured, usually held in the raw formats as this allows trying various modeling techniques and derive an optimal one.

While loading this data, we can use various techniques like **ETL (Extract, Transform, and Load)**, **ELT (Extract, Load, and Transform)**, or **ETLT (Extract, Load, Transform, and Load)**.

- **Extract, Transform, and Load**: It is all about transforming data against a set of business rules before loading it into a data sandbox for analysis.

- **Extract, Load, and Transform**: In this case, the raw data is loaded into a data sandbox and then transformed as a part of analysis. This option is more relevant and recommended over ETL as a prior data transformation would mean cleaning data upfront and can result in data condensation and loss.

- **Extract, Transform, Load, and Transform**: In this case, we would see two levels of transformations:

  - Level 1 transformation could include steps that involve reduction of data noise (irrelevant data)
  - Level 2 transformation is similar to what we understood in ELT

In both ELT and ETLT cases, we can gain the advantage of preserving the raw data. One basic assumption for this process is that data would be voluminous and the requirement for tools and processes would be defined on this assumption.

The idea is to have access to clean data in the database to analyze data in its original form to explore the nuances in data. This phase requires domain experts and database specialists. Tools like Hadoop can be leveraged. We will learn more on the exploration/transformation techniques in the coming chapters.

Phase 4 – model

This phase has two important steps and can be highly iterative. The steps are:

- Model design
- Model execution

In the model designing step, we would identify the appropriate/suitable model given a deep understanding of the requirement and data. This step involves understanding the attributes of data and the relationships. We will consider the inputs/data and then examine if these inputs correlate to the outcome we are trying to predict or analyze. As we aim to capture the most relevant variables/predictors, we would need to be vigilant for any data modeling or correlation problems. We can choose to analyze data using any of the many analytical techniques such as logistic regression, decision trees, neural networks, rule evolvers, and so on.

The next part of model design is the identification of the appropriate modeling technique. The focus will be on what data we would be running in our models, structured, unstructured, or hybrid.

As a part of building the environment for modeling, we would define data sets for testing, training, and production. We would also define the best hardware/software to run the tests such as parallel processing capabilities, and so on.

Important tools that can help building the models are R, PL/R, Weka, Revolution R (a commercial option), MADlib, Alpine Miner, or SAS Enterprise Miner.

The second step of executing the model considers running the identified model against the data sets to verify the relevance of the model as well as the outcome. Based on the outcome, we would need further investigation on additional data requirements and alternative approaches to solving the problem in context.

Phase 5 – publish insights

Now comes the important part of the life cycle, communicating/publishing the key results/findings against the hypothesis defined in phase 1. We would consider presenting the caveats, assumptions, and limitations of the results. The results are summarized to be interpreted for a relevant target audience.

This phase requires identification of the right visualization techniques to best communicate the results. These results are then validated by the domain experts in the following phase.

Phase 6 – measure effectiveness

Measuring the effectiveness is all about validating if the project succeeded or failed. We need to quantify the business value based on the results from model execution and the visualizations.

An important outcome of this phase is the recommendations for future work.

In addition, this is the phase where you can underscore the business benefits of the work, and begin making the case to eventually put the logic into a live production environment.

As a result of this phase, we would have documented the key findings and major insights as a result of the analysis. The artifact as a result of this phase will be the most visible portion of the process to the outside stakeholders and sponsors, and hence should clearly articulate the results, methodology, and business value of the findings.

Finally, engaging this whole process by implementing it on production data completes the life cycle. The following steps include the engagement process:

1. Execute a pilot of the previous formulation.
2. Run assessment of the outcome for benefits.
3. Publish the artifacts/insights.
4. Execute the model on production data.
5. Define/apply a sustenance model.

References/Further reading

- Data analytics life cycle blog by *Steve Todd*: `http://www.innovationexcellence.com/blog/tag/data-analytics-lifecycle/`

- *3D Data Management: Controlling Data Volume, Velocity and Variety, Doug Laney, Gartner*

- Scaling Facebook to 500 Million Users and Beyond by *Robert Johnson*: `http://www.facebook.com/note.php?note_id=409881258919`

Summary

In this chapter, we covered details on understanding enterprise data, its features and categories. We then moved on to define Big Data with the core data definition from enterprise data. We also looked at the paradigm shift that Big Data has brought in and how the market is gearing up to use the technology advancements to handle the Big Data challenges. We also saw how traditional approaches no longer fit the Big Data context and new tools and techniques are being adopted. We also familiarized you with data analytics techniques, their purpose, and a typical data science life cycle.

In the next chapter, we will learn about Greenplum UAP. We will take a deep dive into the differentiating architectural patterns that make it suitable for advanced and Big Data analytics. In terms of hardware as well as software, we would be drilling into each of the modules and their relevance in the current context on analytics in discussion.

2
Greenplum Unified Analytics Platform (UAP)

Now that we understand the context of data science and analytics, let us explore requirements for a platform that helps implement analytics in an agile way. There are many pieces to an analytics project that requires a unified or integrated platform as opposed to a bunch of tools or frameworks.

This chapter elaborates on the architecture and application of Greenplum **Unified Analytics Platform** (**UAP**) in Big Data analytics context. Greenplum UAP combines the capabilities to process structured and unstructured data with a productivity engine and a social network engine that cans the barriers between the data science teams.

The Greenplum UAP solution combines Greenplum Database (an MPP, shared nothing, and analytics optimized relational database competing with data warehousing solutions), HD (a Hadoop distribution with proprietary integration), Greenplum Chorus (an analytics collaboration platform), Greenplum DCA (a flexible appliance for hosting the Greenplum UAP), and administration tools for managing and monitoring platform components. While this chapter introduces you to Unified Analytics Platform, *Chapter 4*, *Implementing Analytics with Greenplum UAP* provides detailed step-by-step guidance on how to use the components, and configure the environment for implementation.

The topics covered in this chapter are listed as follows:

- Need for a unified or integrated platform for Big Data analytics
- Core concepts of analytical data architecture:
    - Data warehousing, OLTP versus OLAP
    - Column-oriented databases
    - Parallel versus distributed processing/computing

- ° Shared nothing data architecture and **massive parallel processing (MPP)**
- ° Elastic scalability
- ° Data loading patterns: ETL versus ELT versus ETLT

- Greenplum UAP, composed of:

  - ° Software/Framework:

    Greenplum Database

    HD (Hadoop)

    Chorus

    Integration with third-party tools

  - ° **Data Computing Appliance (DCA)** modules: database modules, HD modules, and **Data Integration Accelerator (DIA)** modules.

 Greenplum UAP is currently being repositioned by Pivotal. The modules and components are being rebranded to include the "Pivotal" tag and are being packaged under PivotalOne. Few of the VMware products such as GemFire and SQLFire are being included in the Pivotal Solution Suite along with RabbitMQ. Additionally, support/ integration with **CEP (Complex Event Processing)** for real-time analytics is added. Hadoop (HD) distribution, now called Pivotal HD, with new framework HAWQ has support for SQL-like querying capabilities for Hadoop data (a framework similar to Impala from open source distribution). However, the current features and capabilities of the Greenplum UAP detailed in this book will still continue to exist.

Big Data analytics – platform requirements

Organizations are striving towards becoming more data driven and leverage data to gain the competitive advantage. It is inevitable that any current business intelligence infrastructure needs to be upgraded to include Big Data technologies and analytics needs to be embedded into every core business process. The following diagram depicts a matrix that connects requirements from low storage/cost to high storage/ cost information management systems and analytics applications.

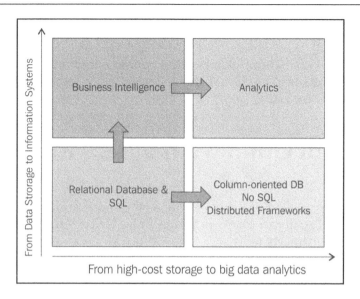

The following section lists all the capabilities that an integrated platform for Big Data analytics should have:

- A data integration platform that can integrate data from any source, of any type, and highly voluminous in nature. This includes efficient data extraction, data cleansing, transformation, and loading capabilities.

- A data storage platform that can hold structured, unstructured, and semi-structured data with a capability to slice and dice data to any degree, discarding the format. In short, while we store data, we should be able to use the best suited platform for a given data format (for example: structured data to use relational store, semi-structured data to use NoSQL store, and unstructured data to use a file store) and still be able to join data across platforms to run analytics.

- Support for running standard analytics functions and standard analytical tools on data that has characteristics described previously.

- Modular and elastically scalable hardware that wouldn't force changes to architecture/design with growing needs to handle bigger data and more complex processing requirements.

- A centralized management and monitoring system.

- Highly available and fault tolerant platform that can repair itself in times of any hardware failure seamlessly.

- Support for advanced visualizations to communicate insights in an effective way.

- A collaboration platform that can help end users perform the functions of loading, exploring, and visualizing data, and other workflow aspects as an end-to-end process.

Greenplum Unified Analytics Platform (UAP)

The following figure gives a one-shot view of all the architectural layers of Greenplum Unified Analytics Platform that includes Greenplum, Hadoop, Chorus, and interfaces to third-party tools:

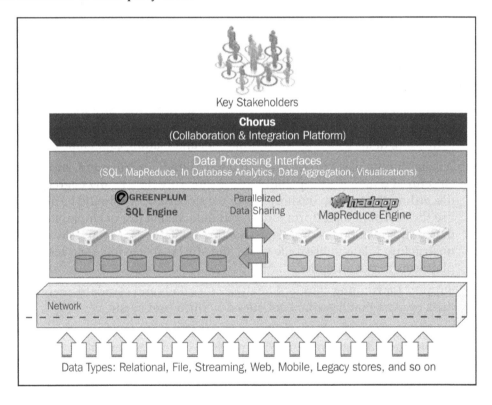

Greenplum's Unified Analytics Platform integrates tools and frameworks that address the preceding requirements and provides a non-monolithic approach to Big Data analytics.

Core components

The following figure depicts core software components of Greenplum UAP:

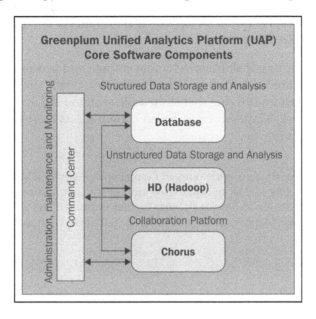

In this section, we will take a brief look at what each component is and take a deep dive into their functions in the sections to follow.

Greenplum Database

Greenplum Database is a shared nothing, massively parallel processing solution built to support next generation data warehousing and Big Data analytics processing. It stores and analyzes voluminous structured data. It comes in a software-only version that works on commodity servers (this being its unique selling point) and additionally also is available as an appliance (DCA) that can take advantage of large clusters of powerful servers, storage, and switches. GPDB (Greenplum Database) comes with a parallel query optimizer that uses a cost-based algorithm to evaluate and select optimal query plans. Its high-speed interconnection supports continuous pipelining for data processing.

 In its new distribution under Pivotal, Greenplum Database is called Pivotal (Greenplum) Database.

Hadoop (HD)

HD stands for Hadoop. This software is a commercially supported distribution of Apache Hadoop. It includes **HDFS (Hadoop Distributed File System)**, MapReduce, and other ecosystem packages from Apache like HBase, Hive, Pig, Mahout, Sqoop, Flume, YARN, and ZooKeeper.

Hadoop is known for its capabilities to handle storage and processing of large volumes of unstructured data (volumes to the degree of petabytes) on commodity servers with its robust underlying distributed file system HDFS, and its parallel processing framework, MapReduce. It is also known for its fault-tolerant and high-availability architecture.

 Some of the new endeavors in Pivotal with Pivotal HD include leveraging HD as an underlying storage for Greenplum Database with a vision to have scalability further improved and an SQL interface to query data from Hadoop (with HAWQ framework).

Chorus

Chorus provides a collaboration platform that helps stakeholders seamlessly access and operate on data used for analytics. It is a social networking portal that helps import, search, explore, visualize, and communicate insights both within and external to the organization. This platform binds Greenplum Database, Hadoop, and many other third-party tools for ETL, visualization, and analytics.

Command Center

Greenplum Command Center acts as a single console for all the components. It provides a set of interactive dashboards that help monitor the health of the application by collecting performance metrics. It shows data on the system/hardware utilization and query performance collected at regular intervals.

Modules

The figure below lists core modules under DCA that host UAP core components discussed in the previous section.

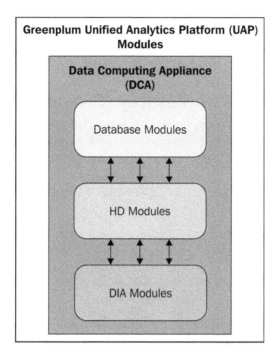

Data Computing Appliance is an advanced hardware solution that is highly scalable. It includes modules for architecturally-integrated database, computing, storage, and network. It offers modular solution for structured data, unstructured data, and partner applications for business intelligence and ETL services. Functionally, DCA helps deliver fast and scalable data loading, data integration, or co-processing for Big Data analytics.

More details on the hardware capacity will be covered in the next sections. The preceding figure depicts Greenplum Unified Analytics Platform Data Computing Appliance and its modules.

Database modules

Analytic database modules of DCA are known to provide infrastructure or hardware to hold Greenplum Database software. There are two flavors of database modules, standard and high capacity that vary on storage and processing capabilities.

HD modules

These modules support traditional Hadoop processing that can operate independently or be integrated with analytic database modules and other third-party partner applications. Each of these modules includes storage, computation, and interconnect. HD modules are available in two flavors too. One that is based on storage and another that is more about compute and is mainly aimed at leveraging Isilon or other off-cluster storage for the HDFS layer.

Data Integration Accelerator (DIA) modules

DIA modules host third-party partner applications for **ETL** (**Extract, Transform, and Load**), **BI** (**Business Intelligence**), analytics (R, MADlib, SAS, and others), and visualization (Tableau and others) solutions. By integrating third-party applications with the DCA using DIA modules. The overall **Total cost of ownership (TCO)** is minimized as we can leverage the 10 Gig network backplane shipped with the appliance.

Core architecture concepts

This section explains some fundamental and architectural concepts underlying Greenplum Unified Analytics Platform solution.

Greenplum Database is a shared nothing, massively parallel processing data warehousing solution that helps handle petabyte scale data with ease. It is built on an open source database, PostgreSQL. It can be physical or virtual, can run on any kind of hardware, and there is a software only version of Greenplum that customers can leverage. As we now understand the characteristics and concept of Big Data, let us next explore the concept of data warehousing.

Data warehousing

This section introduces readers to the concept of data warehousing as well as the basic elements used in building and implementing a data warehouse.

A data warehouse is a consolidation of information gathered about the enterprise. It is a centralized or single point of data reference for enterprise data that usually comes from multiple sources and facilitates ease of access for analysis.

Following are the characteristics of data in a data warehouse:

- **Integrated, centralized, and unique**: Irrespective of the various sources of data in an enterprise, a data warehouse is responsible to hold a single copy of data.

- **Data definition/metadata**: Data warehouse requires a unique data definition supporting data aggregation process. This data now becomes a single version of truth for the enterprise.

- **Relevant and subject-oriented**: Data relevance is identified by its timely availability and historic data to be referenced against the time element. Also, data usually has time dimension.

- **Non-volatile**: Data stored is usually in read-only formats.

- **Security**: Confidential data must be protected against unauthorized access.

The following figure depicts various components of data warehouse architecture:

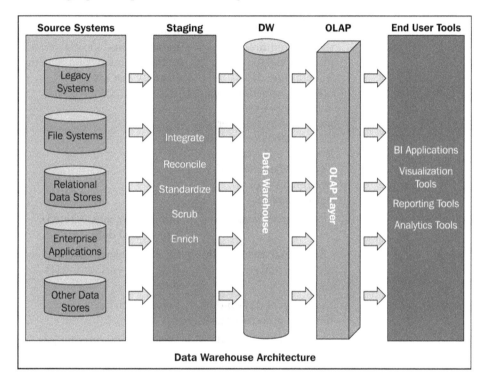

Data Warehouse Architecture

The following table summarizes the differences between typical **OLTP (Online Transaction Processing)** and **OLAP (Online Analytic Processing)** data stores. Greenplum Database is flexible and supports OLTP and OLAP structures.

	OLTP databases	OLAP databases
	Online Transaction Processing databases	Online Analytical Processing databases
Definition	Involves many short online transactions (INSERT, UPDATE, and DELETE). Fast query processing is the core requirement for these databases. Maintaining data integrity, concurrency, and effectiveness measured by number of transactions per second is a basic expectation. Usually characterized by high level of normalization.	Involves relatively low volume of transactions and complex queries involving slicing and dicing of data. Data stored is usually aggregated, historical in nature, and mostly stored in multi-dimensional schemas (usually star schema).
Data type	Operational data.	Integrated/consolidated/aggregated data.
Source	OLTP databases usually are the actual sources of data.	OLAP databases consolidate data from various OLTP databases.
Primary purpose	Execution of day-to-day business processes/tasks.	Serves decision support.
CUD	Short, fast inserts and updates initiated by users.	Periodic long running jobs refreshing the data.
Queries	Usually works on smaller volumes of data, executes simpler queries.	Often complex queries involving aggregations and slicing and dicing on multi-dimensional structure.
Throughput	Usually very fast due to relatively smaller data volumes and quicker running queries.	Usually run in batches and in higher volumes; may take several hours depending on volumes.

	OLTP databases	OLAP databases
Storage capacity	Relatively small as historical data is archived.	Requires larger storage space due to the volumes involved.
Schema design	Highly normalized with many tables.	Typically denormalized with fewer tables; use of star and/or snowflake schemas.
Backup and recovery	Requires rigorous backup religiously; operational data is critical to run the business; data loss is likely to entail significant monetary loss and legal liability.	Instead of regular backups, some environments may consider simply reloading the OLTP data as a recovery method.

Column-oriented databases

Typically, all relational databases are row-oriented, each new row indicates a new data set for the given table structure. Column-oriented data storage, like the name indicates, stores data by its column rather than row. The primary difference lies in the way the hard disk is accessed that results in efficiency. The following screenshot depicts the difference between row- and column-oriented databases:

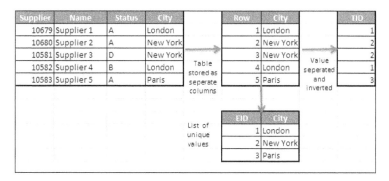

The drawback with the regular row-oriented RDBMS databases is that the number of the rows in a table impacts on the performance of SQL query running on that table. If we look at analytic query requirements, what is usually required is a column and by employing a row-oriented storage, we end up accessing the whole row as the column is locked in its place in a row. In other words, the level of granularity of I/O operations is the record. There are a few techniques to overcome the full table scans, one of which is indexing. But, as we all know, it comes with its own overhead.

With column-oriented databases (also referred to as column stores), the data is decomposed into respective columns and the granularity of I/O access is now the column and this could mean significant gain in query efficiency.

These stores are used for read-intensive data that is large in volume. A high degree of compression can be achieved here and in Greenplum, these tables are by default append-only. In short, column stores can be used in conjunction with row stores as they are complimentary. Whenever a write is required, it is moved into a row store that is later compressed and synchronized or moved into a column store.

In the next sections, we will discuss polymorphic data storage capabilities of Greenplum that helps combine the best of the two worlds in a seamless manner.

Parallel versus distributed computing/processing

Parallel systems have been there for a while now and the new paradigm that has gained traction in the Big Data world is distributed systems. In this section, let us explore how the parallel and distributed systems conceptually compare and contrast.

To understand parallel systems, we will use a simple taxonomy, Flynn's taxonomy (1966). He classified parallel systems using two streams, data streams and instruction streams. The following figure is a representation of Flynn's taxonomy:

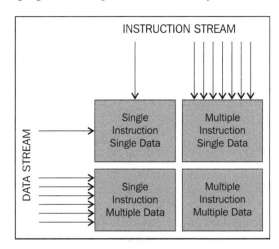

- **Single Instruction Single Data (SISD)**: This is a case of a single processor with no parallelism in data or instructions. A single instruction is executed on single data in a sequential manner. For example, uniprocessor.
- **Multiple Instruction Single Data (MISD)**: In this, multiple instructions operate on a single data stream; a typical example can be fault tolerance.

- **Single Instruction Multiple Data (SIMD)**: This is a case of natural parallelism; a single instruction triggers operation on multiple data streams.

- **Multiple Instructions Multiple Data (MIMD)**: A case where multiple independent instructions operate on multiple and independent data streams. Since the data streams are multiple, the memory can either be shared or distributed. Distributed processing can be categorized here. The previous figure depicts MIMD and a variation in a distributed context.

One of the critical requirements of parallel/distributed processing systems is high availability and fault tolerance. There are several programming paradigms to implement parallelism. The following list details the important ones:

- **Master/workers model**: Master is the driver where the work is held and then disseminated to the workers. Greenplum Database and HD modules implement this pattern. We will learn more about the architecture in the following sections.

- **Producer/consumer model**: Here there is no owner who triggers the work. Producer generates work items, consumer subscribes and executes asynchronously.

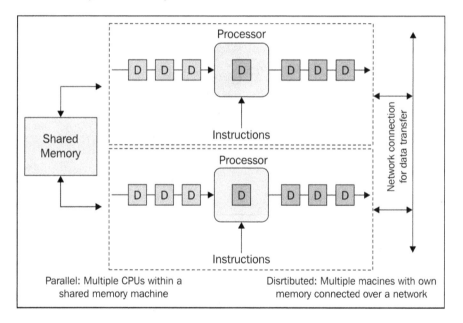

Shared nothing, massive parallel processing (MPP) systems, and elastic scalability

Until now, our applications have been benchmarked for certain performance and the core hardware and its architecture determined its readiness for further scalability that came at a cost, be it in terms of changes to the design or hardware augmentation. With growing data volumes, scalability and total cost of ownership is becoming a big challenge and the need for elastic scalability has become prime.

This section compares shared disk, shared memory, and shared nothing data architectures and introduces the concept of massive parallel processing.

Greenplum Database and HD components implement shared nothing data architecture with master/worker paradigm demonstrating massive parallel processing capabilities.

Shared disk data architecture

Have a look at the following figure which gives an idea about shared disk data architecture:

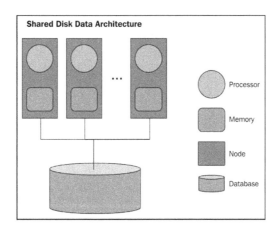

Shared disk data architecture refers to an architecture where there is a data disk that holds all the data and each node in the cluster accesses this data for processing. Any data operations can be performed by any node at a given point in time and in case two nodes attempt persisting/writing a tuple at the same time, to ensure consistency, a disk-based lock or intended lock communication is passed on thus affecting the performance. Further with increase in the number of nodes, contention at the database level increases. These architectures are **write limited** as there is a need to handle the locks across the nodes in the cluster. Even in case of the reads, partitioning should be implemented effectively to avoid complete table scans.

Shared memory data architecture

Have a look at the following figure which gives an idea about shared memory data architecture:

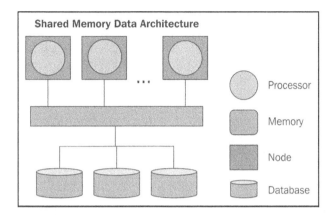

In memory, data grids come under the shared memory data architecture category. In this architecture paradigm, data is held in memory that is accessible to all the nodes within the cluster. The major advantage with this architecture is that there would be no disk I/O involved and data access is very quick. This advantage comes with an additional need for loading and synchronizing data in memory with the underlying data store. The memory layer seen in the following figure can be distributed and local to the compute nodes or can exist as data node.

Shared nothing data architecture

Though an old paradigm, shared nothing data architecture is gaining traction in the context of Big Data. Here the data is distributed across the nodes in the cluster and every processor operates on the data local to itself. The location where data resides is referred to as data node and where the processing logic resides is called compute node. It can happen that both nodes, compute and data, are physically one. These nodes within the cluster are connected using high-speed interconnects.

The following figure depicts two aspects of the architecture, the one on the left represents data and computes decoupled processes and the other to the right represents data and computes processes co-located:

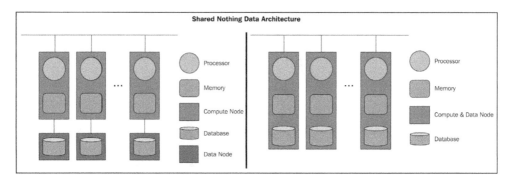

One of the most important aspects of shared nothing data architecture is the fact that there will not be any contention or locks that would need to be addressed. Data is distributed across the nodes within the cluster using a distribution plan that is defined as a part of the schema definition. Additionally, for higher query efficiency, partitioning can be done at the node level. Any requirement for a distributed lock would bring in complexity and an efficient distribution and partitioning strategy would be a key success factor.

Reads are usually the most efficient relative to shared disk databases. Again, the efficiency is determined by the distribution policy, if a query needs to join data across the nodes in the cluster, users would see a temporary redistribution step that would bring required data elements together into another node before the query result is returned.

Shared nothing data architecture thus supports massive parallel processing capabilities. Some of the features of shared nothing data architecture are as follows:

- It can scale extremely well on general purpose systems
- It provides automatic parallelization in loading and querying any database
- It has optimized I/O and can scan and process nodes in parallel
- It supports linear scalability, also referred to as elastic scalability, by adding a new node to the cluster, additional storage, and processing capability, both in terms of load performance and query performance is gained

Data loading patterns

From what we have learned about data warehousing, it is very evident that data loading forms a major process. This process is responsible for pulling data from various source systems and consolidating it into a warehouse.

The data loading function is beyond just extracting and loading data. It involves data scrubbing, transformation, and cleansing processes that should be driven using configurable business rules and requires a standard data definition/metadata in place. In this section, we will explore various data loading patterns that can be considered for implementing complex transformations (transformations that are done on higher volumes of data and require frequent lookups of data references from the underlying database).

There are three alternatives that can be considered for deciding on where the transformation or data scrubbing logic should reside.

- **Pattern 1, Extract, Transform, and Load** (ETL): This is the case where the transformations are done within the data integration tier and the final data is pushed onto the target (database).

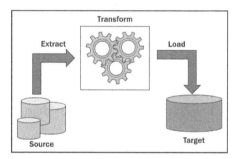

- **Pattern 2, Extract, Load, and Transform** (ELT): In this case the data is loaded in an efficient manner onto the target (database) and the entire transformation is done at the target.

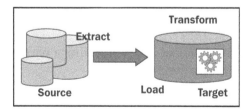

- **Pattern 3, Extract, Transform, Load, and Transform (ETLT)**: This is a combination of the previous two alternatives, where we choose to leverage all the in-built transformation and scrubbing functions of Informatica and go to the target for all complex transformations that might/might not involve large volumes.

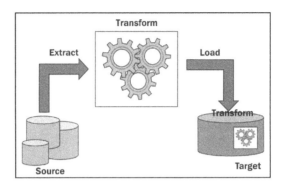

Most of the data integration tools in the market (including Informatica PowerCenter) support a feature called **Pushdown Optimization (PDO)**. The Pushdown Optimization technique helps achieve optimal performance by load balancing the processing across the servers. Let us take an example of transformation logic that requires filtering of data based on a condition that requires to lookup data from the database table with a large number of rows. Instead of loading data onto the data integration tier and processing the filter logic, running an SQL query on the database could prove to be optimal. This is the case where the transformation logic is pushed down to be executed at the target database level rather than at the source. This is the ELT case.

Before we examine the suitable data loading pattern, we would need to consider the following points:

- Identify if data load throughput is a crucial requirement
- Estimate the current workload on the source and target platforms
- Measure the cost of hardware and software to add additional computing resources to the target environment
- Guesstimate relative efficiency of performing a particular operation in the source, target, or integration system

The following table provides a comparative analysis of the proposed data loading patterns:

	ETL	ELT	ETLT
Full form	Extract, Transform, and Load.	Extract, Load, and Transform.	Extract, Transform, Load, and Transform.
Overview	A traditional technique for moving and transforming data in which an ETL engine that is separate from either the source or target DBMS performs the data transformations.	This is a technique for moving and transforming data from one location and format to another instance and format. In this style of integration, the target DBMS becomes the transformation engine	In this technique transformations are partly done by the ETL engine and partly pushed to the target DBMS.
Highlights	• Heavy work of transformation is done within ETL engine. • Uses in-built transformation functions. • Transformation logic can be configured through GUI. • Supported by Informatica.	• Heavy work of transformations is handed over to the DBMS layer. • Transformation logic runs closer to the data. • Supported by Informatica.	• Transformation work is split between the ETL engine and the DBMS. • Facilitates application. • Supported by Informatica.

	ETL	ELT	ETLT
Benefits	• Easy GUI-based configuration. • Transformation logic is independent of and outside the database and is reusable. • Works very well for granular, simple function-oriented transformations that do not require any database calls. • Can run on **SMP** (**Symmetric Processing**) or MPP hardware.	• Leverages RDBMS engine hardware for scalability. • Keeps all data in the RDBMS all the time. • Is parallelized according to the data set and disk I/O is usually optimized at the engine level for faster throughput. • Scales as long as the hardware and RDBMS engine can continue to scale. • Can achieve 3x to 4x the throughput rates on the appropriately tuned MPP RDBMS platform.	• Can balance/ share the workload with the RDBMS.
Risks	• Requires higher processing power on the ETL side. • Higher costs. • Complex transformations that would need reference data would slow down the process.	• Transformation logic is tied to database. • Transformations that involve smaller volume and simple in nature would not gain much benefit.	• Would still have a part of the transformation logic within database.

Greenplum has external tables that support high-speed data loading demonstrating data loading ELT pattern. `gpload` and `gpfdist` utilities are leveraged to load data into the external tables.

Greenplum UAP components

In this section, we will take a deep dive into all the components and modules of Greenplum UAP.

Greenplum Database

Greenplum Database is a collection of several PostgreSQL database instances acting as one interconnected database using highly-tuned optimizer. It is an MPP shared nothing database that involves more than one node to cooperate to execute one operation. Every node has its own disk, memory, and operating system. Greenplum uses this high-performance system architecture to distribute the load of large volume of data warehouses and is able to use all of the system resources in parallel to process a query.

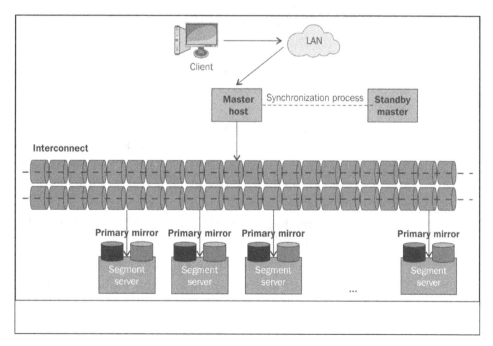

Greenplum Database is based on PostgreSQL 8.2.15 and is very similar with respect to SQL support, features, configuration options, and so on (additionally, features from PostsgreSQL 8.3 and 9.0 have been included). The internals of PostgreSQL have been modified or supplemented to support the parallel structure of Greenplum DB. The interconnect component enables communication between the distinct PostgreSQL instances and makes the system behave as a single logical database. Greenplum DB also includes features designed to optimize Postgres for BI and DW such as external tables (parallel data loader), resource management, and query optimization enhancements.

The Greenplum Database physical architecture

A Greenplum environment or cluster consists of master host, standby master, segment nodes, and interconnect.

The master host is responsible for coordinating the query workload across the segment hosts. The master does not store user data. Standby master is a warm standby master. Segment host runs one or more segment instances. Basically, each segment host runs its own GPDB. Segment hosts run in a **shared nothing** environment with their own CPU, disk, and memory. Segments store data and are responsible for executing queries in parallel. The interconnect between the segment hosts is a high-speed bus or interconnect, pipelining data between the segment hosts. More on each of the components is explained as follows:

- **Master host**:
    - The master host is the entry point to the Greenplum Database system. Users connect to the master and interact with the database as in the case of any other DBMS.
    - Internally runs a Postgres listener process (called Postgres) responsible for getting users connected to the database sessions. By default, this process runs on the port 5432 (daemon process).
    - Master host holds all the system and admin utilities used for administration tasks.
    - Responsible for creating query plans and distributing the workload across all segment nodes.
    - Also responsible for final data aggregations sometimes.
    - It holds the metadata and is never responsible for holding the actual data.

○ The master may perform final processing for queries, for example, aggregations, summations, orders, and sorts. The master does not contain user data. It is also important to note that system and database administration tasks are performed on the master host. The parser checks syntax, semantics, and produces a parse tree for the query optimizer.

The following figure shows master host and its core functions:

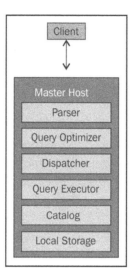

Master host core functions are listed as follows:

Consumption of the parse tree and production of the query plan (query plan contains how the query is executed, for example, hash join versus merge join)

Communication of the query plan to segments

Allocation of cluster resources required to perform the job and accumulating/presenting final results

 A query executor (worker process) is responsible for completing its portion of work and communicating its intermediate results to the other worker processes. For each slice of the query plan, there is at least one worker process assigned. A worker process works on its assigned portion of the query plan independently. During query execution, each segment will have a number of worker processes working on the query in parallel. Related worker processes across segments that are working on the same portion of the query plan are referred to as **gangs**.

- **Standby master**: The standby master is a warm standby server that is activated when the master host is unavailable.

- **Node or segment host**: Node is the server that has the actual installation of Greenplum Database (primary and mirror segments instances).

  ○ Each segment holds a portion of data for each distributed table and index.

  ○ Every segment server can hold multiple segment instances residing on it. By default, there would be one primary segment and if mirroring is enabled, it would have one or more mirrors. By definition, number of primary and mirror segments equal to the number of physical cores.

  ○ Segment servers are not directly accessed by users; all communications with the segments are through the master. Another way to connect is in utility mode (a rare case).

  ○ Each segment instance has PostgreSQL segment listener process (called Postgres). The port numbers are assigned for this process during the segment initialization.

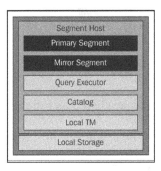

- **Interconnect**: As a portion of work is completed, tuples flow up the query plan from one gang of processes to the next. This interprocess communication between the segments are transmitted through the interconnect. It is a standard Ethernet fabric using UDP protocol by default. UDP provides better performance and scalability. Alternately, TCP can be used by changing the `gp_interconnect_type` from GUC to TCP.

 Pivotal added additional packet verification and checking which is not performed by UDP so the reliability is equivalent to TCP.

- Interconnect is the connection layer between individual database instances, master, and segments. It is the glue that holds all of the components together.

- It is responsible for moving data between the segments during query execution.

- Usually configured as a private LAN; segment servers are not meant to be visible outside the Greenplum array.

- Consists of Gigabit Ethernet network/fiber switch. (In DCA, the interconnect is a 10Gig Ethernet switch. This is a standard recommendation though there is support for other capacities switch.)

- Has gNet software installed.

- **Client programs**: Greenplum Database uses the same client interfaces as PostgreSQL. The following clients are recommended for usage:

  - **psql**: SQL editor shipped with PostgreSQL.

  - **pgAdmin3**: Graphical user interface from PostgreSQL developers.

  - **ODBC drivers**: Postgres ODBC driver psqlODBC.

  - **JDBC drivers**: Postgres JDBC driver pgJDBC.

  - **Python**: PyGreSQL is a famous python interface for Postgres.

  - **libpq**: Native C application programming interfaces for Postgres. These libraries are shipped with Greenplum Database.

  - **Perl DBI**: Perl database interface API to connect Perl programs with Greenplum Database.

 There are new workbenches/tools in the market now; one of the workbenches that is widely used is Aginity.

The Greenplum high-availability architecture

In addition to primary Greenplum system components, we can also optionally deploy redundant components for high availability and avoiding single point of failure.

The following components need to be implemented for data redundancy:

- **Mirror segment instances**: A mirror segment always resides on a different host than its primary segment. Mirroring provides you with a replica of the database contained in a segment. This may be useful in the event of disk/hardware failure. The metadata regarding the replica is stored on the master server in system catalog tables.

- **Standby master host**: For a fully redundant Greenplum Database system, a mirror of the Greenplum master can be deployed. A backup Greenplum master host serves as a warm standby in cases when the primary master host becomes unavailable. The standby master host is synchronized periodically and kept up-to-date using transaction replication log process that runs on the standby master to keep te master host and standby in sync. In the event of master host failure the standby master is activated and constructed using the transaction logs.

- **Dual interconnect switches**: A highly available interconnect can be achieved by deploying redundant network interfaces on all Greenplum hosts and a dual Gigabit Ethernet. The default configuration is to have one network interface per primary segment instance on a segment host (both the interconnects are by default 10Gig in DCA).

High-speed data loading using external tables

Data loading into Greenplum Database can come through an ETL host connected to the interconnect. `gpfdist` utility can be leveraged to connect to external ETL and load data into segments simultaneously using the scatter-and-gather method. This utility runs an internal HTTP light server. The query execution plan is to broadcast to all segments, even if they do not contain data. The segments would then run the query plan with appropriate data. This work is done in parallel.

External tables are used to access data external to the Greenplum Database. Large amounts of data can be loaded or unloaded using external tables. Following formats are supported by external tables:

- **CSV (Comma Separated Values)**, regular file based (`file://`)
- Hadoop file system data (`gphdfs://`)
- Web based external sources with support for text data. (`http://`)

External table types

Greenplum supports two kinds of external tables:

- Readable or read-only tables used for data loading.
- Writable or write-only tables used for data unloading. A writable external table allows selecting rows from database tables and output the rows to files.

Polymorphic data storage and historic data management

Polymorphic data storage is a unique and differentiating feature of Greenplum. It facilitates configuring optimal storage, compression, and execution settings to support row/column-oriented storage and retrieval. As a core requirement for a data warehousing application, we would need to store and process large volumes of data that can be historic in nature.

Partitions need not be the same size or orientation. They can be column or row oriented. We can partition data based on a selected time frame.

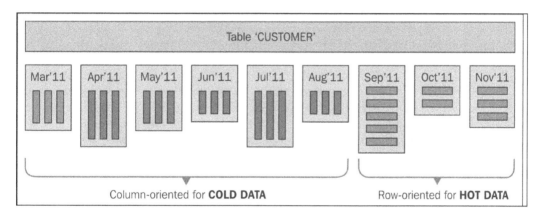

The example shows a rolling management scheme, where three months of data is maintained at a time. The scheme is as follows:

- Anything more than three months is moved to deep history (probably a compressed (most likely) column-oriented store), as per the previous figure
- All in-between months are maintained at a second level of storage (a row-oriented store)

The options can be compressed or uncompressed as well. This process is customizable based on organizational needs and for the user, the data access would be seamless and does not require user's intervention for managing the internals of the storage.

Data distribution

Let us now understand how Greenplum stores data across various hosts and segment instances.

All tables in Greenplum are distributed. This means a table is divided into non-overlapping sets of rows or parts. Each part resides on a single database known as a segment within the Greenplum Database system. The parts are distributed evenly across all of the available segments using a sophisticated hashing algorithm.

Distribution is determined at the table creation time by selecting a distribution key of one or more columns. The distribution key is usually the primary key or any unique column.

In a distributed architecture of this sort, there can be data skew or computational skew. It is important that we select a distribution key with unique values and high cardinality; we should also ensure that it will not result in computational skew.

With respect to high cardinality, typically boolean keys, for example, True/False or Y/N, are not suitable for a distribution key as they will be primarily distributed to two segment instances. In an MPP environment overall response time for a query is dependent on the completion time for all segment instances.

There are two types of distribution policies that help divide rows among the available segments:

- **Hash distribution**: In this distribution technique, one or more table columns are used as the distribution key. These columns are used by the hashing algorithm to divide data among all of the segments. The key value is hashed, or a random number is created. There are performance advantages to choosing a hash policy whenever possible. The largest performance advantages come into play when joining two tables that use the same distribution key. In this case the system does not have to shuffle data between nodes to do a join.

- **Round robin distribution**: When no distribution key is defined, this algorithm is used. In this case, rows are sent to the segments as they come in. This mechanism is usually used for smaller tables.

Hadoop (HD)

In order to handle the analytics for unstructured data, Greenplum UAP provides a commercial version of Apache Hadoop. The HD distribution is integrated with Greenplum Database and supports parallel analytics.

Hadoop is a framework that allows for distributed processing of large unstructured data sets across clusters of commodity servers. It can store a large amount of data and process the large amount of data stored.

Hadoop is originally an open source Apache Project that is implemented in Java.

The following figure depicts two core components of Hadoop:

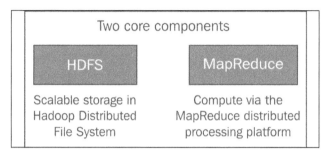

Following are a few important characteristics of Hadoop framework:

- Runs on commodity servers, with elastic scalability; the storage servers and disks are not assumed to be highly available or reliable
- Uses replication strategy to address high availability and reliability requirements
- **Metadata driven design**: Master server called NameNode holds the metadata and the slave nodes called DataNode store data and can handle data processing as well
- Focus here is mostly sequential access with single writes and limited or no file locking features
- Comes with an in-built foolproof fault-tolerant and high-availability architecture

Hadoop Distributed File System (HDFS)

The figure below depicts HDFS architecture with the associated daemons:

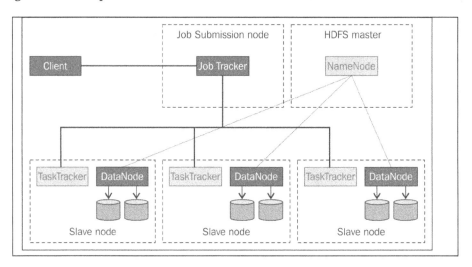

HDFS architecture follows master-slave architecture paradigm. The master node is referred to as NameNode and has the following functions:

- File system namespace management
- File name to list blocks and location mapping details maintenance
- Block allocation/replication management
- Checkpoints namespace and journals namespace changes for reliability
- Access control to namespace
- DataNodes are the salves with the following functions:
    - Blocks storage using the underlying OS's files
    - Access to the blocks is given to the clients directly from DataNodes
    - Communication of status and health to the NameNode periodically
    - Checks for block integrity periodically

Hadoop MapReduce

Hadoop MapReduce function and flow is depicted in the following figure. There are a series of functions that are executed within the MapReduce flow **Mapper | Combiner | Partitioner | Shuffle and Sort | Reducer**. Few of the functions in the flow can be implicit (have a default behavior, if not coded for).

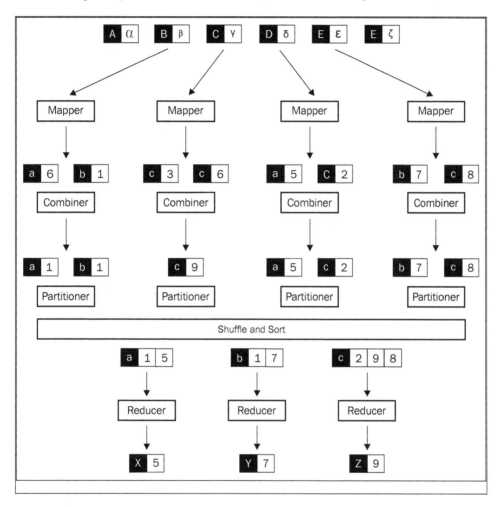

Hadoop enables the data scientists to create MapReduce jobs quickly and efficiently. The screenshot below shows **Greenplum Command Center** with database and HD modules installed.

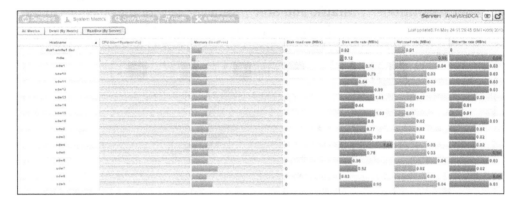

Chorus

Chorus is a collaborative platform in Greenplum UAP that supports self-service analytic infrastructure. With Chorus, organizations can extract data insights with ease and communicate across stakeholders.

Chorus allows defining, publishing, and sharing new insights, and maintaining a live library of insights.

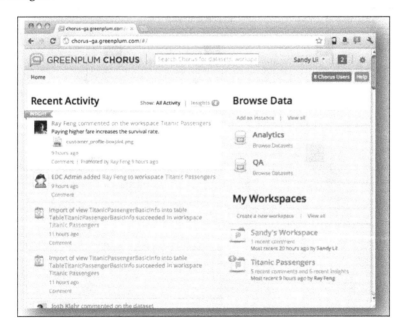

It provides integration with third party BI, ETL, and analytical tools. It facilitates analytical workflows to effectively communicate results over time.

It provides interface to browse all the data sources, use in-built visualization tools to derive insights, and share the data sets with the teams.

Greenplum Data Computing Appliance (DCA)

Greenplum Data Computing Appliance (DCA) is a purpose-built, highly scalable parallel data warehousing appliance. The DCA:

- Brings the processing power of MPP architecture
- Delivers fastest data loading capacity
- Provides flexible and linearly scalable infrastructure to support growing business needs

There are two flavors of expandable rack configuration provided by DCA:

- Greenplum Database Standard Module
- Greenplum Database High Capacity Module provides increased storage with no increase in footprint

The appliance approach is beneficial as it eases implementation with overall lower total cost of ownership, ensures scalability, high availability, and fault tolerance.

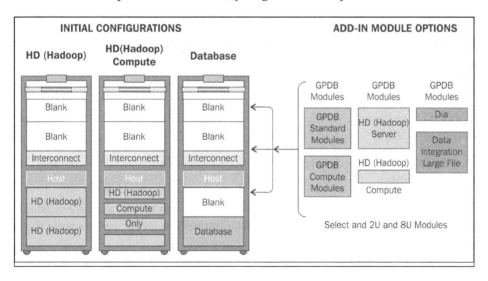

DCA UAP surpasses the previous release with more CPU cores, more RAM, more spindles per rack. Hardware specific details are:

- Master, DIA, and HD compute servers are constructed on the E5-2660 CPU, 64 GB RAM, and 6 x 300 GB 10K SAS drives

- GPDB compute servers are constructed with the same processor and amount of RAM as the masters, DIA, and HD compute servers, but include 24 x 300 GB 10K SAS drives

- GPDB standard servers use the same processor and memory configuration, but with 24 x 900 GB 10K SAS drives

- HD servers have 12 x 3 TB 7K SATA drives

Attribute	Master, DIA, HD compute server	GPDB compute server	GPDB standard server	HD server
CPU	E5-2660 2, 1G, 95W	E5-2660 2, 1G, 95W	E5-2660 2, 1G, 95W	E5-2660 2, 1G 95W
DIMM	8 x 8 GB	8 x 8 GB	8 x 8 GB	8 x 8 GB
Drive capacity	6 x 300 GB	24 x 300 GB	24 x 900 GB	12 x 3 TB
Drive interface	10K SAS	10K SAS	10K SAS	7K SATA
Full rack usable capacity, TB, uncompressed	1.8 TB raw each server	41	124	188

Greenplum Data Integration Accelerator (DIA)

Greenplum DIA is an open systems integrator that architecturally integrates all the tools and frameworks within Greenplum. This module is optional and can be integrated into DCA.

DIA has built-in support for external data sources. An external ETL is usually integrated into this.

For example, Informatica PWX connector for Greenplum works directly within DIA and can load large volumes of data into Greenplum using gpfdist via the high-speed interconnect.

References/Further reading

- Greenplum Database administration guide: `http://media.gpadmin.me/wp-content/uploads/2012/11/GPDBAGuide.pdf`

- Greenplum Command Center guide: `http://www.greenplumdba.com/greenplum-command-center-features-and-references`

- Getting started with Hadoop: `http://hadoop.apache.org/docs/stable/index.html`

- Cloudera Hadoop tutorial: `http://www.cloudera.com/content/cloudera-content/cloudera-docs/HadoopTutorial/CDH4/Hadoop-Tutorial.html`

- Hadoop MapReduce tutorial: `http://hadoop.apache.org/docs/stable/mapred_tutorial.html`

Summary

In this chapter, we covered Greenplum UAP, its various components, and its modules. We have also been introduced to some important architectural patterns and concepts underlying Greenplum analytics platform. We have also seen how Greenplum ensures high availability and facilitates fault tolerance.

In the next chapter, we shall learn advanced analytics techniques and associated tools. An introduction to R, Weka, and MADlib libraries will be given with a detail on how these integrate with Greenplum UAP.

3
Advanced Analytics – Paradigms, Tools, and Techniques

Welcome to the world of analytics!

In this chapter, we will learn and recap important analytic techniques or methods that data scientists employ and practice as a part of a data science project implementation. For each of the analytic techniques, we will set the context for its application and detail the expected outcome. Additionally, we will learn how to apply R, Weka, MADlib, and Hadoop frameworks and tools for analytics in general as well as in the context of Greenplum.

The following topics are covered in this chapter:

- Introduction to standard analytic paradigms: descriptive, predictive, and prescriptive analytics
- Dive deep into important analytical methods: simulations, clustering, data mining, text analytics, decision trees, association rules, linear and logistic regression, and so on
- Technology and tools:
    - R programming
    - Weka
    - In-database analytics using MADlib

Analytic paradigms

The following figure depicts the journey of data from being mere data to bringing business insights for competitive advantage and various analytic paradigms driving the transformation:

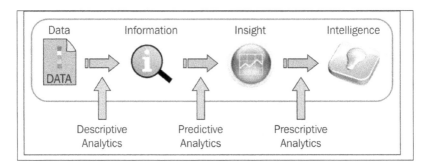

The purpose of analytics is to derive actionable insights from data, helping make smarter decisions, and thus bringing in competitive advantage for an organization. The approach we take to architect and design strategies to derive these insights varies. It is very important that organizations have an optimal data warehouse / business intelligence (BI) architecture in place that can efficiently ingest and analyze large and diverse data sets.

Here are three paradigms of data analytics:

- Descriptive analytics
- Predictive analytics
- Prescriptive analytics

Descriptive analytics

Descriptive analytics is all about taking data and analyzing past actions for intuitions to help identify an approach for the future. Historical data related to past failures or success is collected and mined/processed for the actual reasoning behind a success or failure.

The variable that is measured is usually referred to as a dependent variable and all other variables that determine its value or state are referred to as independent variables. Every independent variable in data is analyzed to identify its relationship with the dependent variable. For example, a customer buying or not buying a fitness product is determined by factors such as BMI, demographic details, and age. Here, buying or not buying of the fitness product is the dependent variable and all the factors that determine this decision are the independent variables.

This analysis can be categorized as a post-mortem process and involves collection of quantitative data, and usually provides hindsight that can be used for future or predictions.

Descriptive models quantify dependencies and relationships in data in a way that is often used to categorize prospects. Descriptive modeling techniques focus on all aspects of the data as against a single outcome and simulate all possible dependencies. Some descriptive models and statistics do make assumptions about the data being measured. For example, the assumption that the data set is normally distributed, or that the data set is linear.

An example outcome of descriptive models is categorizing customers by their product preferences and age. Example methodologies for this categorization are classification and clustering. We will learn more about it in the following sections. As a next step to this categorization, descriptive models can help model a large number of individual elements and help make predictions.

Predictive analytics

Predictive analytics is all about turning data into valuable and actionable information. Predictive analytics employs all the attributes of data analyzed as a part of descriptive analytics to conclude a probable future outcome, given a situation context.

Predictive analytics paradigm includes running a variety of statistical techniques to analyze historical and current behavior to make predictions about future events.

Predictive models can identify and exploit specific customer patterns to determine possible risks and opportunities, given a particular condition or context. The following are the three important aspects of predictive analytics:

- Modeling
- Decision analysis
- Optimization and profiling

Let us look at some examples where predictive analytics can be used:

- **Customer relationship management systems**: Using predictive analytic techniques, we can analyze the entire customer data, identify patterns, and predict their behavior.

- **Product management and sales**: For a company that offers multiple products, we can use predictive analytics to analyze the spending patterns of customers and identify cross sales or additional sales, thus paving way to higher profitability. This is also referred to as cross-selling or up-selling.

It is important that a strong team of business or domain experts and data scientists is formed who understands statistical modeling techniques and can apply these on data to derive business insights. The problems that we are solving and the questions we are answering are based on the needs of the business, which typically are not of statisticians or data scientists.

Prescriptive analytics

Prescriptive analytics is a little beyond deriving data insights and can go to an extent of suggesting options on probable decisions to be taken. It takes advantage of the predictive analytics and applies, for example, machine learning techniques to suggest the best suited action and presents the quantifiable business implications of each possible decision and action.

While predictive analytics stops at anticipating what will happen and when it will happen, prescriptive analytics goes a little beyond and additionally anticipates why it will happen.

For every new occurrence of an event in business, prescriptive analytics takes advantage of the new data and uses it to improve the accuracy or confidence of the prediction and thus provide optimal decision alternatives.

Prescriptive analytics, like any other analytic approaches, operates on data that can be structured or unstructured in nature. It includes application of business rules and implied mathematical models that could include machine learning and natural language processing techniques. Here are a few important examples where prescriptive analytics is used for deriving business edge:

- Fluctuating gas prices can impact manufacturing costs of manufacturing companies. Using prescriptive analytics, statistical modeling, and mathematical trending, future gas prices can be predicted and decisions on the course of action to tap the best gas price can be taken, thus helping lower overall manufacturing costs.

- Prescriptive analytics can be used in healthcare, helping hospitals to strategically plan the growth by analyzing economic data, population demographic trends, and population health trends.

Analytics classified

In this section, we will focus on learning all the popular analytical techniques that come under one of the discussed paradigms: descriptive, predictive, and prescriptive analytics.

- Classification
- Forecasting or prediction or regression
- Clustering
- Optimization
- Simulations

These analytic techniques can perform either of the two:

- Supervised analysis
- Unsupervised analysis

Supervised analysis is a case where the data is known to us. Client also defines a specific goal for our analysis and in case of unsupervised analysis, the data might be known to us, but we usually do not start with a definitive target in mind.

Classification

Classification is all about identifying a grouping technique for a given dataset in such a way that depending on a value of the target attribute, the entire dataset can be qualified to belong to a class. This is one of the techniques used in data mining to identify the data behavior patterns.

Let's take an example, a marketing manager looking at his customer data wants to identify if a given customer is helping him make profits and take a decision on if it's worth spending effort and time on the customer demands. This is commonly referred to as Total Lifetime Value (TLV).

We have the data and we start by plotting on a graph as shown in the following figure (the one on the left) not really worrying about what this plotting would mean. On the y-axis, we have the total money spent (in multiples of hundreds of rupees) and on the x-axis, we have the number of items purchased. As a next step, we categorize the data on the graph into good and bad customers, for example. In the following graph, all the customers who spend more than 800 rupees in a single purchase are categorized as good customers (this is a hypothetical example or analysis).

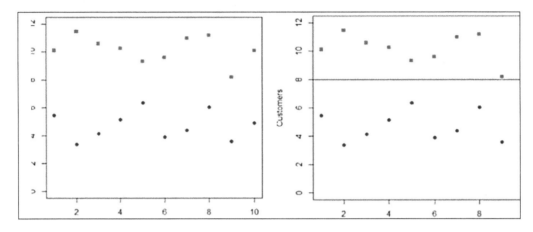

From the next time onwards, the marketing manager can plot the new customers on this graph and based on which side they fall, predicting whether the customer is likely to be good or bad.

Note that classification need not always be binary (yes or no, male or female, good or bad, and so on). Any number of classifications is feasible (poor, below average, average, above average, or good) based on the problem definition. Also, note that in regression what you are finding is a continuous value and in classification, it takes only a few values.

This analytical procedure is referred to as supervised learning as the data on which we operate is known to us and the expectation on what needs to be analyzed from the data is defined.

Forecasting or prediction or regression

Forecasting or prediction is all about the way things would happen in future. This information can be derived from past experience or knowledge. In this case, we can have little data and through regression we end up defining the future. Forecasting and prediction results are usually presented along with the degree of uncertainty.

Let us take an example here. We have an agriculture scientist working on a new crop that she developed. As a trial, this seed was planted at various altitudes and yield was computed. Once we plot a graph between yield and altitude, the relationship between both the parameters is identified and the capability on predicting the yield at any other altitude is gained. You can observe that the data usually does not perfectly fit a line, and once the line is fit and the equation is noted (of course along with errors), we can get rid of the data. This technique is called regression.

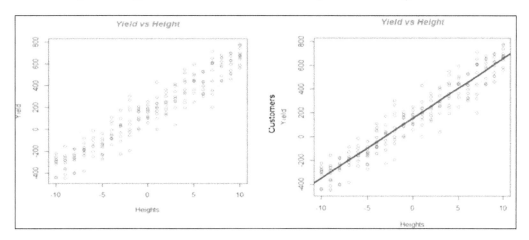

Clustering

Most of the time, the data analyst is just given some data and is expected to unearth interesting patterns that may help in deriving intelligence. The main difference between this task and that of a classification is that, in the classification problem, the business user specifies what he/she is looking for (a good customer or a bad customer; a success or a failure, and so on).

Let us consider the same example as we did in the *Classification* section. In clustering, the patterns to classify the customers are identified without any target in mind or any prior classification. When running a classification given a specific model, the results will always be the same, whereas with clustering, it may not be the same (for example, depending on how the initial centroids are picked). An example modeling method for clustering is K-means clustering. You may learn more on K-means in the following section.

To summarize, clustering is a classification analysis, where we do not start with a specific target in mind (good/bad; will buy/will not buy), and hence referred to as unsupervised analysis.

Optimization

Optimization, in simple terms, is a mechanism to make something better or define a context for a solution that makes it the best.

Let us take an example of a production scenario. There are two machines that produce the desired product; but one machine requires more energy with a high speed in production and lower raw materials, while the other requires higher raw materials and lesser energy to produce the same output within the same time. It is important to understand the patterns in the output based on the variation in inputs; a combination that gives highest profits would probably be the one, the production manager would want to know. You, as an analyst, will identify the best possible way to distribute the production between the machines that gives him the highest profit. The below figure shows a point of highest profit when a graph was plotted for various distribution options between the two machines, the goal of this technique is to identify this point.

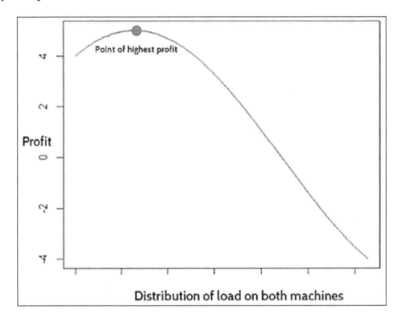

Simulations

In addition to all the techniques we defined until now, there might be situations where the data in context itself has a lot of uncertainty. For example, a project manager is given a task and she can estimate with her prior knowledge that the team can perform the task in 2-4 hours.

The cost of input material may vary between $100-150 and the number of employees who come to work on any given day may be between six and nine. An analyst then estimates how much time the project might take. Solving such problems requires simulating a vast amount of alternatives.

Typically, in forecasting, classification, and unsupervised learning, we are given data and we really do not know how the data is interconnected. There is no equation to describe one variable as a function of others. In optimization, we have the relation well defined and we also have access to data. In simulations, we do have a well-defined relation. But, the input data itself is uncertain.

Essentially, data scientists combine one or more of the above techniques to solve challenging problems.

- Web search and information extraction
- Drug design
- Predicting capital market behavior
- Understanding customer behavior
- Designing robots

Modeling methods

In the next few sections, we will cover the following important analytical methods in detail:

- Decision trees (classification)
- Association rules (unsupervised learning)
- Linear and logistic regression
- Naive Bayesian classifier (classification)
- K-means clustering (unsupervised learning)
- Text analysis.

Decision trees

Decision trees are an example of classification technique. Here, we classify data in a tree format using data features or attributes. Since decision trees depict the flows and possible outcome for each flow, they are used in identifying the best strategy to reach the goal.

In decision trees, we start with testing an attribute and split the data based on that attribute:

- We continue with the process.
- We can build multiple decision trees for the same problem.
- The efficiency and size of the tree is directly proportional to the attributes chosen by us.
- We also need to have termination criteria:

    ○ One obvious criterion is that all the records at the node belong to one class and hence cannot be split.

    ○ A significant majority of records belong to a single class (say, if 99 percent records are buyers, we are fine).

    ○ The segment contains only one or a very small number of records.

    ○ The improvement is not substantial enough to warrant making the split. If we do not terminate at the right place, we might overfit the data.

    ○ We can read a decision tree as a rule. Each branch connects nodes with "and" and multiple branches are connected by "or".

    ○ It divides up the data on each branch point without losing any of the data (the number of total records in a given parent node is equal to the sum of the records contained in its two children).

    ○ Most importantly, the outputs are simple rules and are extremely easy to understand by the business users. You may also build some intuitions about your customer base. For example, "Are customers with different family sizes truly different?".

It turns out that we are collecting very similar records at each leaf. So, we can use median or mean of the records at a leaf as the predictor value for all the new records that obey similar conditions. Such trees are called regression trees.

Decision trees are robust to errors, both errors in classifications of the training examples and errors in the attribute values that describe these examples. Decision tree methods can be used even when some training examples have unknown values (for example, if the age is known for only some of the training examples). Every starting or terminating point in a decision tree is called a *node* and the connections between nodes are *branches*.

There are three types of nodes and two types of branches in decision trees of data mining:

- Nodes:
    - ° **Decision node**: A decision node is represented by a square and represents a point in the tree where a decision needs to be taken.
    - ° **Event node**: An event node represents a point where the choice of option ends. Event nodes are represented by a circle.
    - ° **Terminal node**: These nodes represent the final outcome for every flow and this is where the tree ends.
- Branches:
    - ° **Decision branch**: These branches are the connections that start from a decision branch and connect to an event or decision or a terminal node
    - ° **Event branch**: These branches connect an event node to another event or decision or terminal node

The following figure shows the standard decision tree representation using relevant notations:

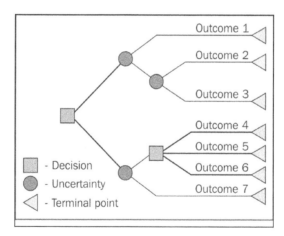

In the image below, the decision tree representation helps analyze if a street shop vendor should set up his stall outdoors or indoors depending on the weather conditions. This decision tree is based on a prediction clause that has 50 percent possibility for a sunny day, 15 percent possibility for rain, and 35 percent possibility for a cloudy day. A rough estimation on what the vendor would earn in a day if he has his stall outside versus inside is as shown. The overall earnings are computed to be $102.5 for a stall outside versus $46 for a stall inside. It can be concluded that the shopkeeper should have his stall outside and probably hope no rains for the day.

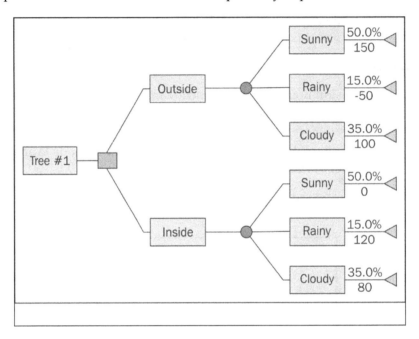

In decision trees, to identify the attributes that form an important part of decision making, we calculate entropy, Gini index, information gain, and reduction in variance (we will not deal with details on these techniques in this book).

There are two most popular techniques that help identify the most relevant attribute in a given data set:

- **CART** (regression and classification tress): These trees are for binary representation, which means every node can have a maximum of two outcomes. Gini index is used for identification of the impacting attributes.

- **C4.5**: Decision trees that use this technique can have more than two outcomes and thus multiple binary trees can be created. Due to the inherent complexity involved, there are a few important pruning techniques like information gain that helps in the most relevant attribute selection.

Association rules

Association rules is a classification technique and is all about finding patterns that occur frequently, defining associations, or correlations among sets of items. This technique is applied in market basket analysis, cross-marketing, catalog design, and so on. The following image depicts a rule and formulas for support, confidence, and lift associated:

$$Support = \frac{frq(X,Y)}{N}$$

$$Rule: X \Rightarrow Y \longrightarrow Confidence = \frac{frq(X,Y)}{frq(X)}$$

$$Lift = \frac{Support}{Supp(X) \times Supp(Y)}$$

Let us now look at an example to understand how association rules technique works.

The following table presents a list of items that have been bought by the customers of a supermarket (each line represents a single purchase by a customer):

Customer Number	Items
1	Bread, Peanuts, Milk, Fruit, and Jam
2	Bread, Jam, Soda, Chips, Milk, and Fruit
3	Steak, Jam, Soda, Chips, and Bread
4	Jam, Soda, Peanuts, Milk, and Fruit
5	Jam, Soda, Chips, Milk, and Bread
6	Fruit, Soda, Chips, and Milk
7	Peanuts, Soda, Fruit, and Milk
8	Cheese, Peanuts, Yogurt, and Fruit

From a given transaction as above, we will now work to understand if an occurrence of one item in the table is driven by the presence of any other item in the same transaction.

Some of the associations that we can derive are:

- {Bread} => {Jam}
- (Soda} => {Chips}
- {Bread} => {Milk}

These denote implications of the form X => Y, where X and Y are **itemsets**.

Let us now get acquainted with some terminology used in the context of association rules.

- **Itemset**: A collection of one or more items is called an itemset. An example of an itemset from the preceding table is {Milk, Bread, Jam}.
    - k-itemset is an itemset that has k items

- **Support (s)**: Support is the fraction of transactions that contain an itemset. For example:

    s({Milk, Bread}) = 3/8

    s({Chips, Soda}) = 4/8

- **Support count (σ)**: Support count denotes the frequency of occurrence of an itemset.

    σ ({Milk, Bread}) = 3

    σ ({Chips, Soda}) = 4

- **Confidence (c)**: Confidence measures how often an itemset occurs in a transaction that has another itemset.

    c = σ ({Milk, Bread}) / σ ({Bread }) = 0.75

Let us take binary partitions of an itemset {Milk, Bread, Jam}. The following lists the support and confidence for each of the association rule identified:

- {Bread, Jam} => {Milk} s= 0.4, c= 0.75
- {Milk, Jam} => {Bread} s= 0.4, c= 0.75
- {Bread} => {Milk, Jam} s= 0.4, c= 0.75
- {Jam} => {Bread,Milk} s= 0.4, c= 0.6
- (Milk}=> {Bread, Jam} s= 0.4, c= 0.5

Rules that have same itemset usually have same support, but can have different confidence.

The association rules technique follows a two-step approach:

1. Identify and generate frequent itemsets.
2. Generate high-confidence rules from frequent itemsets.

Identifying frequent itemsets can be computationally intensive. For a given number of items, say n, we can gave 2^d itemsets. The following image depicts itemset definition for five items.

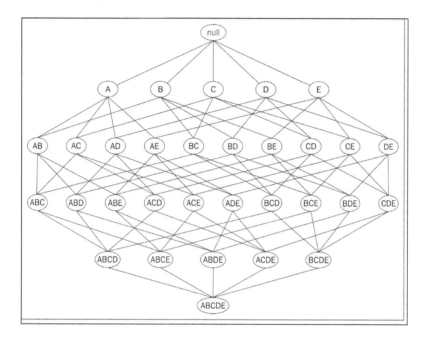

One of the frequent itemset generation strategies is to reduce number of candidates by pruning (using Apriori algorithm).

The Apriori algorithm

Apriori is one of the ancient and the most commonly used algorithms for association rules. Apriori algorithm uses the notion of frequent itemset.

For example, if we define L as an itemset (L = {Bread, Jam}), we define our support to be 50 percent (s = 50%).

If 50 percent of the transactions have the itemset L, we say L is a frequent itemset.

It is apparent that if 50 percent of itemsets have {Bread, Jam} in them, at least 50 percent of the transactions will have either {Bread} or {Jam} in them.

Apriori algorithm principle is that a subset of frequent itemset also is frequent.

In Apriori approach, we often start bottom-up, we start with all the frequent itemsets of size 1 (for example, Bread, Jam, Milk, and so on) first and determine the support. Then we start pairing them. We find the support for, say {Bread, Jam} or {Jam, Milk} or {Milk, Bread}.

The following figure shows an illustration of the pruning done as a result of an Apriori algorithm:

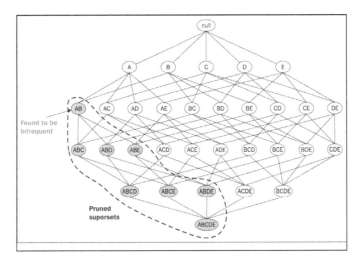

The output of the Apriori is the rules with minimum support and confidence.

The following figure depicts Apriori pruning on the preceding example:

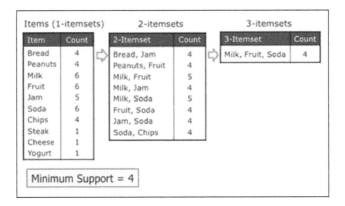

For more measures refer to http://michael.hahsler.net/research/association_rules/measures.html.

Linear regression

Regression techniques help fit an equation given in the dataset. The idea of fitting an equation is to enable prediction for a variable in the equation driven by a change in any other variable and understand any impact of a variable over the other. Here, for similar decision trees, we would have dependent and independent attribute or variables.

Regression techniques thus can be used for prediction, estimation, modeling relationships, or hypothesis testing. The following figure shows a standard representation and the terminology used:

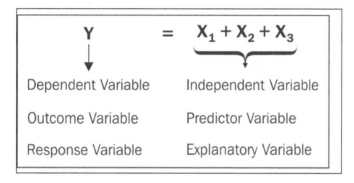

When we want to model a dependent variable Y as a function of three different independent variables (X1, X2, and X3), we usually would not have enough data to estimate the relationship or the function, and hence we start with an assumption of linear dependency. Here, most of the effort is in studying variables that are deterministically related to each other.

The following is a representation of linear probabilistic regression model:

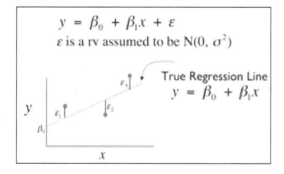

The limitations are:

- Linear regression does not handle the missing values well. It assumes that each variable affects the outcome linearly and additively. So, if we have some variables that affect the outcome nonlinearly and the relationships are not actually additive, the model does not fit well.

- It is recommended to take the log of monetary amounts or any variable with a wide dynamic range. It cannot handle variables that affect the outcome in a discontinuous way.

- Also, when we have discrete drivers with a large number of distinct values the model becomes complex and computationally inefficient.

Logistic regression

Logistic regression is the preferred method for many binary classification problems. For example:

- True/false
- Approve/reject
- Buy/don't buy

Logistic regression is apt if we need the probability of an event against predicting class variables. It is recommended that we try logistic regression in the first step for all binary class problems. In a logical regression model, the outcome is determined by a process like flipping a coin. The predictors that we know determine the process, but the unknown determines the outcome here. Hence, we determine what change in predictor changes the probability of the outcome.

Logistic regression is also called logit model. An example for logistic regression model is analyzing the factors that influence winning or losing in an election for a politician. The dependent variable would be binary, win, or lose and the predictor variables of interest can be the amount of money and time spent on the campaign, demographic conditions of the candidate, and so on.

In a logistic function, as the response variable is binary, there is a curved relationship seen in the plotting and this is referred to as **sigmoid**. The following figure shows four variants of sigmoid curves (we can observe that the value for **y** oscillates between 0 and 1):

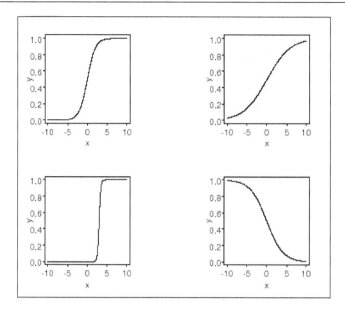

The Naive Bayesian classifier

Often all of machine learning algorithms need to be modeled for supervised learning tasks such as classification and prediction, or for unsupervised learning tasks like clustering.

To understand the concept of Naive Bayes classification, let us start with an example:

The need here is to classify a new customer as "green" or "red" based on the analysis done on the existing customers. Let us look at the existing plotting as shown in the following figure:

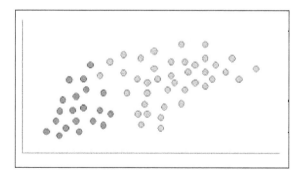

Since there are twice as many good customers (green) plotted as bad (ones in red), it is reasonable to believe that a new customer who hasn't yet been evaluated is twice as likely to be green rather than red. In the Bayesian analysis, this belief is known as the prior probability. Prior probabilities are based on previous experience and in the current example, the percentage of green and red plotted. As the word indicates, it is often used to predict outcomes before they actually happen. Let us now assume there is a total of 60 customers, with 40 of them classified as good and 20 of them as bad. Our prior probabilities for class membership are:

- *Prior probability of good customers: number of good customers (40) / total number of customers (60)*

- *Prior probability of bad customers: number of bad customers (20) / total number of customers (60)*

Having formulated our prior probability, we are now ready to classify a new customer (white circle in the following figure). We then calculate the number of points in the circle belonging to each class label. From this we calculate the likelihood of the new customer to be marked as good or bad.

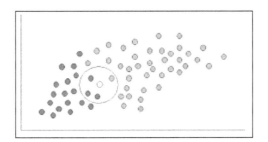

K-means clustering

K-means clustering algorithm is considered one of the simplest unsupervised learning techniques. As a first step, the given data is classified into a set of fixed k clusters. Every cluster would have its own centroid placed carefully and away from each other. As a next step, a unique point in a cluster is associated to the nearest centroid. This exercise is done until all the points identified are exhausted.

Based on these associations, new centroids are identified. A repeat of the preceding exercise is done until no changes or movements in the centroids are identified. Finally, this algorithm aims at minimizing an objective function; in this case, a squared error function.

This is more iterative and a nonhierarchical method for data classification.

Text analysis

Text analysis is essentially the processing and representation of data that is in text form for the purpose of analyzing and learning new models from it.

The main challenge in text analysis is the problem of high dimensionality. When analyzing a document, every possible word in the document represents a dimension.

The other major challenge with text analysis is that the data is unstructured.

The process or the problem-solving tasks in text analysis is composed of three important steps namely parsing, search/retrieval, and text mining.

Parsing is the process step that takes the unstructured or semi-structured document and imposes a structure for the downstream analysis. Parsing is basically reading the text which could be weblog, an RSS feed, an XML or HTML file, or a Word document. Parsing decomposes what is read in, and renders it in a structure for the subsequent steps.

Once parsing is done, the problem focuses on search and/or retrieval of specific words or phrases or in finding a specific topic or an entity (a person or a corporation) in a document or a corpus (body of knowledge). All text representation takes place implicitly in the context of the corpus. All search and retrieval is something we are used to performing with search engines such as Google. Most of the techniques used in search and retrieval originated from the field of library science.

With the completion of these two steps, the output generated is a structured set of tokens or a bunch of keywords that were searched, retrieved, and organized. The third task is mining the text or understanding the content itself. Instead of treating the text as a set of tokens or keywords, in this step we derive meaningful insights into the data pertaining to the domain of knowledge, business process, or the problem that we are trying to solve.

Many of the techniques that we mentioned in the previous sections such as clustering and classification can be adapted to the text mining, with the proper representation of the text. We could use K-means clustering or other methods to tie the text into meaningful groups of subjects. Sentiment analysis and spam filtering are examples of a classification tasks in text mining (recall that we listed spam filtering as a prominent use case for Naïve Bayesian classifier). In addition to the traditional statistical methods, natural language processing methods are also used in this phase.

It should be noted that the list of tasks are not ordered. One generally starts with the parsing, either with the intention of compiling them into a searchable corpus or catalog (maybe after some analytical tasks such as tagging or categorization), or specifically for the purpose of text mining. So it's not a process, it's a set of things that go into the text analysis task. Or maybe a tree, where you start with parsing, and go down to either search or to text mining

R programming

This section focuses on onboarding the readers to R programming. Details on installation and sample programs are provided as a part of this section for reference.

R is a scripting language for statistical data analysis and exploration. It was inspired by the statistical language S developed by AT&T. S later was sold to a small firm, which added a GUI interface and named the result S-Plus. SAS and MATLAB are other popular data analysis environments. It is a tool for data manipulation that includes connecting to data sources and slicing and dicing data, data modeling, and visualizations.

The use of R is increasing exponentially in the predictive analytics community.

Of course, the biggest attraction with R is that it is open source, fairly powerful (comparable to the commercial packages), and is flexible (available on Windows, Linux, and Mac).

Let us get started with installation. Windows users visit `http://cran.rproject.org/bin/windows/base/` and install the latest version.

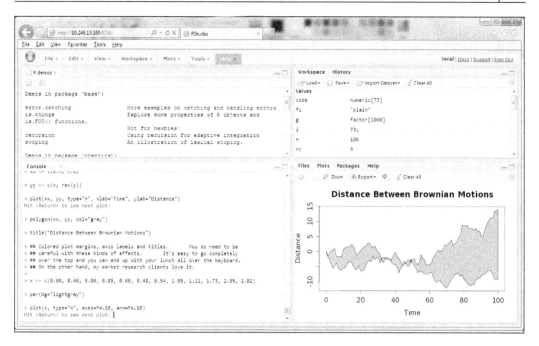

At its simplest, R can be used as a simple calculator shown as follows:

```
> 2.12983*3.87654
[1] 8.256371
> 7%%3
[1] 1
> 7%/%3
[1] 2
> round(8.554987,3)
[1] 8.555
>
```

R provides wonderful built-in help. The following figure shows data types that are supported by R:

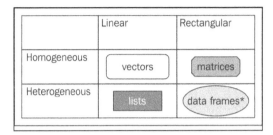

Have a look at the following example:

```
> example(seq)

seq> seq(0, 1, length.out=11)
 [1] 0.0 0.1 0.2 0.3 0.4 0.5 0.6 0.7 0.8 0.9 1.0

seq> seq(stats::rnorm(20)) # effectively 'along'
 [1]  1  2  3  4  5  6  7  8  9 10 11 12 13 14 15 16 17 18 19 20

seq> seq(1, 9, by = 2)      # matches 'end'
[1] 1 3 5 7 9

seq> seq(1, 9, by = pi)     # stays below 'end'
[1] 1.000000 4.141593 7.283185

seq> seq(1, 6, by = 3)
[1] 1 4

seq> seq(1.575, 5.125, by=0.05)
 [1] 1.575 1.625 1.675 1.725 1.775 1.825 1.875 1.925 1.975 2.025 2.075 2.125 2.175
[14] 2.225 2.275 2.325 2.375 2.425 2.475 2.525 2.575 2.625 2.675 2.725 2.775 2.825
[27] 2.875 2.925 2.975 3.025 3.075 3.125 3.175 3.225 3.275 3.325 3.375 3.425 3.475
[40] 3.525 3.575 3.625 3.675 3.725 3.775 3.825 3.875 3.925 3.975 4.025 4.075 4.125
[53] 4.175 4.225 4.275 4.325 4.375 4.425 4.475 4.525 4.575 4.625 4.675 4.725 4.775
[66] 4.825 4.875 4.925 4.975 5.025 5.075 5.125

seq> seq(17) # same as 1:17, or even better seq_len(17)
 [1]  1  2  3  4  5  6  7  8  9 10 11 12 13 14 15 16 17
```

In quite a few simulations, we need to generate random numbers. R has a comprehensive library of functions to do this. Use `runif` to generate multiple random numbers uniformly between two numbers. Have a look at the following example:

```
runif(1, 2, 3)
runif(10, 5.0, 7.5)
```

Of course, every time you get a different number. The sample function generates an integer random number between numbers:

```
sample(1:10, 5, replace=T)
```

The first argument is a vector of valid numbers to generate (here, the numbers are 1 to 10), the second argument indicates numbers to be returned, and the third argument states that once a number is generated, R can still use that number in future generations. So, a true there means you may see the same random number more than once. The default is `replace=F`. In such cases, there will not be a repetition.

The most basic data type in R and is called a **Vector**.

The following commands show a set of interesting operations on vectors:

```
x=seq(1, 1000, by=2)
y=seq(2, 1000, by=2)
z=c(x,y)
length(z)
mean(x)
median(y)
sd(y)
max(x)
min(y)
sort(z)
summary(z)
```

The `rep` command is used for repeating values, shown as follows:

```
> rep(5,50)
 [1] 5 5 5 5 5 5 5 5 5 5 5 5 5 5 5 5 5 5 5 5 5 5 5 5 5 5 5 5 5 5 5 5 5 5 5 5 5 5 5 5 5
[42] 5 5 5 5 5 5 5 5
> rep(1:3,6)
 [1] 1 2 3 1 2 3 1 2 3 1 2 3 1 2 3 1 2 3
> rep(1:3,c(6,6,6))
 [1] 1 1 1 1 1 1 2 2 2 2 2 2 3 3 3 3 3 3
> rep(1:3,rep(6,3))
 [1] 1 1 1 1 1 1 2 2 2 2 2 2 3 3 3 3 3 3
> rep(c(1,2),c(4,4))
 [1] 1 1 1 1 2 2 2 2
```

There are many other important data types in R like lists and data frames that are used abundantly. This book just introduces to the concept of R programming. In the next section, we will implement Monte Carlo simulations using R programming.

When there is a lot of randomness in the inputs, it is very difficult to compute output precisely, even though the output-input relation is simple and well established. In such a case:

1. Generate randomly one possible outcome with one possible set of inputs.

2. Repeat it large number of times.

3. Take the average or summary statistic.

Let us work out a number of trivial and not so trivial problems to illustrate the usefulness of the approach.

Let us start with computing the value of pi. While nobody computes pi using this method, it gives a fairly good view of how the Monte Carlo method works.

If the radius of the circle in the preceding figure is r, the area of the quarter circle = $\frac{\pi r^2}{4}$, and area of the square enclosing the circle is r2.

$$Value\ of\ pi = \frac{4 * area\ of\ the\ quarter\ circle}{area\ of\ the\ enclosing\ square}$$

Imagine a thought experiment where you build this quarter circle and square on a large canvas and you throw darts. If you throw sufficient darts, the ratio of darts that fall within the circle are proportional to the area of the circle. Same is the case with the square.

The r code is provided in the electronic format. The results are:

```
For 10 simulations, pi = 3.2
For 100 simulations, pi = 3
For 1000 simulations, pi = 3.004
For 1e+05 simulations, pi = 3.14028
For 1e+06 simulations, pi = 3.14284
```

The following figure illustrates examples of a few visualization capabilities in R:

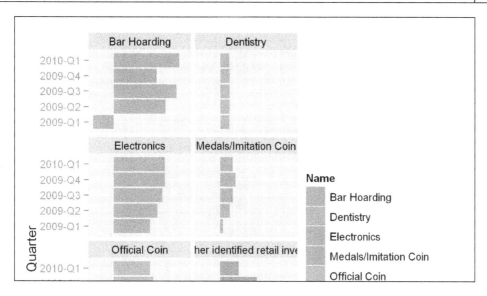

Weka

Weka stands for **Waikato Environment for Knowledge Analysis**. It is a Java-based tool for data mining and machine learning built by the University of Waikato. The mining algorithms can directly be applied onto the data sets or can be run from the Java code. It has tools for data preprocessing, regression, clustering, classification, and many other techniques with a capability to visualize.

Visit `http://www.cs.waikato.ac.nz/~ml/weka/index.html` for more details.

Key features of Weka are listed below:

- 49 data preprocessing tools
- 76 classification/regression algorithms
- Eight clustering algorithms
- Three algorithms for finding association rules
- 15 attribute/subset evaluators and 10 search algorithms for feature selection

The tool primarily has three user interfaces:

- **Explorer**
- **Experimenter**
- **KnowledgeFlow**

The following figure shows Knowledge Explorer user interface from where navigation to various functions for preprocessing, classification, clustering, association rules, and visualizations is available under different tabs.

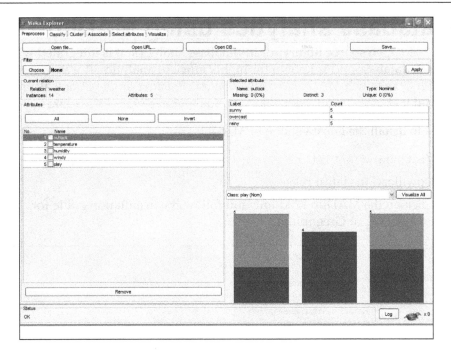

The following figure depicts a sample visualization that can be executed in Weka:

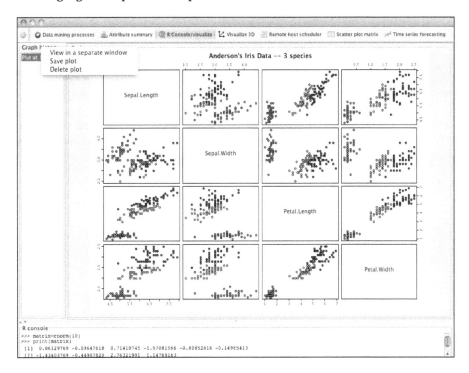

In-database analytics using MADlib

MADlib is an open source library for in-database analytics. It is integrated with Greenplum database and is known for highly efficient analytics. It was first reported at VLDB 2009 in which *MAD Skills: New Analysis Practices for Big Data* was presented. Read about it at `http://db.cs.berkeley.edu/papers/vldb09-madskills.pdf`.

The steps to install the latest version of MADlib are:

1. Visit `http://MADlib.net`.
2. Download the latest release.
3. Click on the MADlib Wiki link and follow the installation guide for PostgreSQL or Greenplum.

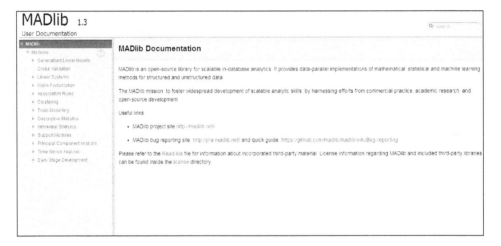

Listed are the in-database analytic functions available natively in Greenplum and as Madlib functions (MADlib functions in bold). This list keeps expanding with every update and as the user community contributes to the MADlib.

Descriptive Statistics	Modeling
Quantile	Association Rule Mining
Profile	K-means Clustering
CountMin (Cormode-Muthukrishnan) Sketch-based Estimator	Naive Bayes Classification
FM (Flajolet-Martin) Sketch-based Estimator	Linear Regression
MFV (Most Frequent Values) Sketch-based Estimator	Logistic Regression
Frequency	Support Vector Machines
Histogram	SVD Matrix Factorization
Bar Chart	Decision Trees/CART
Box Plot Chart	Neural Networks
Correlation Matrix	Parallel Latent Dirichlet Allocation

References/Further reading

- MADlib: www.madlib.net

- R tutorial: http://cran.r-project.org/doc/manuals/R-intro.html

- Weka documentation and tutorial: http://www.cs.waikato.ac.nz/ml/weka/documentation.html

Summary

In this chapter, we have learnt key analytics paradigms: descriptive, predictive, and prescriptive analytics. We have taken a dive deep into few key advanced analytical methods.

The focus of this chapter has been to introduce to R programming, Weka, and in-database analytics using MADlib. At the end of this chapter, readers should be able to identify relevant tools that can be used in the context of analytic problem statement. In the next chapter, an explanation on using these tools with Greenplum is given with examples; and other advanced SQL techniques for in-database analytics in the context of Greenplum will be detailed.

4
Implementing Analytics with Greenplum UAP

In this chapter we will focus on actual implementation of the core tasks in data science life cycle using Greenplum analytics platform. As a quick recap, let us look at all that we covered until now. We have defined characteristics of Big Data, requirements for the next generation analytics, and business intelligence platform. We have also learnt about various phases of data science life cycle, and understood all that Greenplum has to offer to address the analytics' requirements. We have covered a little theory on some standard analytical methods and have had a quick onboarding exercise for R, Weka, and MADlib frameworks. We now have analytics' requirements and we also know where Greenplum product suite can be leveraged.

Let's now look at the implementation using Greenplum Products. We will also look at integration between various components.

This chapter covers the following topics:

- Data loading
    - Structured (into Greenplum)

        Using Greenplum loading utilities in combination with external tables

        Using external ETL tool (like Informatica; we will cover using Informatica's PWX Connector for Greenplum for high-speed data loading)

    - Unstructured data (into Hadoop)

- Using Greenplum data loaders to load data into **Hadoop Distributed File System (HDFS)**
  - ° Loading data from Hadoop (HDFS) into Greenplum

- Data unloading from Greenplum and Hadoop environments
- Querying and reporting data
  - ° Querying Greenplum
  - ° Querying **Hadoop (HD)**
  - ° Querying Greenplum and Hadoop (combining structured and unstructured data)

- Greenplum **Data Computing Appliance (DCA)** and monitoring
- Running analytic functions
  - ° R and Weka with Greenplum
  - ° Advanced SQL options on Greenplum for analytics (Windows functions and aggregates)
  - ° MADlib with Greenplum

- Using Chorus

Data loading for Greenplum Database and HD

This section provides step-by-step instructions on all the approaches to load structured data into Greenplum Database (ELT using external tables) and any unstructured data into HD using proprietary utilities within Greenplum distribution. Additionally, for Greenplum Database, we will also look at options to integrate with an external ETL tool like Informatica PowerCenter using a specialized connecter called **PowerExchange(PWX)** connector.

Greenplum data loading options

Data can be loaded, transformed, and formatted in Greenplum using in-built utilities and tools. There are the options that load data into Greenplum in parallel or sequential form. The following are the different ways to load data into Greenplum Database:

- **INSERT**: INSERT command is a standard SQL command that is used for loading data into database tables in a row-by-row fashion. This option should not be used for loading large columns. In this option, data is routed through the master node and can prove to be a bottleneck in case of large volumes. This command is commonly used in JDBC/ODBC-based communication.

  ○ Syntax:

```
INSERT INTO <<table_name>> (<<column names list separated by
commas>>) VALUES (<<corresponding values>>);
```

  ○ Example:

```
INSERT INTO employee (id, firstname, lastname) VALUES (001,
'John', 'Grisham');
```

- **COPY**: COPY command is one of the initial ways of loading data. It is not parallelized, but is typically used in case of loading large volumes of data and we can run multiple copy commands concurrently. It facilitates copying data from STDIN or STDOUT using the connection between the master node and the client. Given the fact that it can handle volumes and can be manually run concurrently, it is much easier and quicker compared to the other options discussed below.

  ○ Example:

```
COPY employees FROM '/usr/home/historicemployees.dat' WITH
DELIMITER '|';
```

- **External tables**: External tables are unique to Greenplum and are typically used for high-speed, parallel, and bulk loading. External tables access file-based data using file:// or gpfdist:// protocols and dynamic sources can be accessed via http:// protocol. More details on external tables are covered in the next section.

- **gpload**: gpload is a wrapper utility for external tables that internally uses a load specification in a YAML formatted control file. More details in gpload utility are covered in a separate section below.

Before starting to detail available options of loading data for Greenplum Database, let us take a dive deep into Greenplum's external tables. Greenplum has built-in ETL capabilities and we can load and unload data using Greenplum's external tables. The following figure depicts the data loading process that involves loading data via the master node. Both INSERT and COPY commands follow this route.

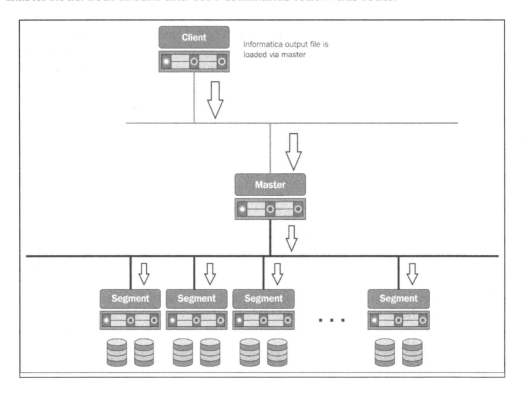

External tables

External tables in Greenplum refer to those database tables that help Greenplum Database access data from a source that is outside of the database. We can have different external tables for different formats. Greenplum supports fast, parallel, as well as nonparallel data loading and unloading. The external tables act as an interfacing point to external data source and give an impression of a local data source to the accessing function.

File-based data sources are supported by external tables. The following file formats can be loaded onto external tables:

- Regular file-based source (supports Text, CSV, and XML data formats): file:// or gpfdist:// protocol

- Web-based file source (supports Text, CSV, OS commands, and scripts): `http://` protocol

- Hadoop-based file source (supports Text and custom/user-defined formats): `gphdfs://` protocol

Following is the syntax for the creation and deletion of readable and writable external tables:

- To create a read-only external table:

```
CREATE EXTERNAL (WEB) TABLE LOCATION (<<file paths>>) |
  EXECUTE '<<query>>' FORMAT '<<Format name for example:
    'TEXT'>>' (DELIMITER, '<<name the delimiter>>');
```

- To create a writable external table:

```
CREATE WRITABLE EXTERNAL (WEB) TABLE LOCATION (<<file
  paths>>) | EXECUTE '<<query>>' FORMAT '<<Format name for
    example: 'TEXT'>>' (DELIMITER, '<<name the
      delimiter>>');
```

- To drop an external table:

```
DROP EXTERNAL (WEB) TABLE;
```

Following are the examples on using `file://` and `gphdfs://` protocol:

```
CREATE EXTERNAL TABLE test_load_file ( id int, name text,
date date, description text )
LOCATION (
'file://filehost:6781/data/folder1/*',
'file://filehost:6781/data/folder2/*'
'file://filehost:6781/data/folder3/*.csv'
)
FORMAT 'CSV' (HEADER);
```

In the preceding example, data is loaded from three different file server locations; also, as you can see, the wild card notation for each of the locations can be different. Now, in case where the files are located on HDFS, the following notation needs to be used (in the following example, the file is ' | ' delimited):

```
CREATE EXTERNAL TABLE test_load_file ( id int, name text,
date date, description text )
LOCATION (
'gphdfs://hdfshost:8081/data/filename.txt'
) FORMAT 'TEXT' (DELIMITER '|');
```

For file-based loading, we can also leverage gpfdist protocol that provides best performance. Details on gpfdist and its usage are covered in a separate section in the later part of this chapter.

Some applications of external tables are as follows:

- Execute queries on external data
- Eliminate badly formatted rows using single row error isolation strategy
- Perform ETL load and data unloads

Greenplum Database has readable and writable external tables:

- **Readable external tables**: They are used for loading data and support basic extraction, transformation, and loading (ETL) tasks for data warehousing. Greenplum Database segment instances read external table data in parallel to optimize large load operations. Data in these tables cannot be modified.
- **Writable external tables**: They are used for unloading data from Greenplum Database. Writable external tables perform the following:
  - Fetch data from database tables into writable external table
  - Connect to another database or ETL to load data elsewhere
  - Export data into files, named pipes, or trigger other executables
  - Interpret output from Greenplum parallel MapReduce process
  - Writable external tables allow only INSERT operations

Important points to consider while handling external tables in Greenplum are as follows:

- When defining an external table, the table and the columns are named just like any other table.
- Add WEB clause to define a WEB external table.
- We use one of the following protocols to access external table data sources. A mix of protocols in the CREATE EXTERNAL TABLE statements is not allowed.
  - **gpfdist**: It points to a directory on the file host or ETL host and loads all external data files into Greenplum primary segments in parallel
  - **gpfdists**: It provides a secure gpfdist
  - **file://**: It is used to access external data files on a segment host that the only super user (gpadmin) can access
  - **gphdfs**: It points to files on the HDFS

- The SEGMENT REJECT LIMIT clause is used to define criteria for single row error handling. If we do not specify this clause, it would mean all or nothing, a complete failure when the first failure is encountered.

- FORMAT is used to define the format (for example, TEXT or CSV).

- In case of DROP EXTERNAL (WEB) TABLE, only the table definition is dropped and the source data is not disturbed.

Web external tables in Greenplum are used to handle dynamic data sources. Web external tables can either be command-based or URL-based.

Command-based web external tables are the tables that get data based on the output of a shell script or command. The command or script must reside on the hosts and should be specified within the EXECUTE clause.

By default, the command is run on all segment hosts and in every segment instance. We can control the number of segment instances we would like to have the command run. The ON clause lists the hosts on which the command needs to be run.

An example is shown as follows:

```
CREATE EXTERNAL WEB TABLE test_output
(id int, name text)
EXECUTE '/tmp/load_scripts/get_test_data.sh' ON HOST
FORMAT 'TEXT' (DELIMITER '|');
```

URL-based web tables get data from the web tables using HTTP protocol.

The LOCATION clause is used to define the list of files on a web server using http:// protocol. The web data files are expected to be accessible to the Greenplum segment hosts.

There can be many URLs specified and the number of URLs correspond to the number of URLs specified, and this corresponds to the number of segment instances that work in parallel to access the web table.

The following is an example command to create a web external table from many URLs:

```
CREATE EXTERNAL WEB TABLE test_table (id int, name text, date
  date, description text)
LOCATION (
'http://abc.com/test1/file.csv',
'http://abc.com/test2/file.csv',
'http://abc.com/test3/file.csv'
)
FORMAT 'CSV' ( HEADER );
```

The following sections will explain different ways of loading data into Greenplum.

gpfdist

The gpfdist protocol provides the best parallel performance. It is a utility in Greenplum and can be easily installed. gpfdist is responsible for ensuring optimal usage of segments while running reads for external table. This utility is run on the server where the external files are located. It can be used similar to the file:// protocol shown in the preceding section to load the data into a regular external table from a file source.

For example, the following command demonstrates loading data from text files that are available on a remote server having gpfdist running on the ports 8081 and 8082 respectively:

```
CREATE EXTERNAL TABLE test_table (id int, name text, date date,
    description text) LOCATION ( 'gpfdist://localhost:8081/*.txt',
      'gpfdst://localhost1:8082/*.txt') FORMAT 'TEXT' (DELIMITER '|'
        );
```

gpfdist can uncompress gzip and bzip2 files by default.

To maximize the performance of gpfdist, following are a few points we should consider.

As the number of segments increases, overall parallel processing should be maximized. We can look at splitting the large file into smaller chunks, typically of similar size, and share them across all the gpfdist locations. Run gpfdist on as many interfaces as possible (and be aware of bonded NICs and be sure to start enough gpfdist to work them). Work should be distributed even across all these resources. In an MPP shared nothing environment, load speed as much as the speed of the slowest node. Any skew in the load file layout will cause the overall load to bottleneck on that resource.

The gp_external_max_segments configuration controls maximum number of segments each gpfdist serves. It gives a number that segments can access external files in parallel. Default value for this parameter is 64. It is important that we keep an even factor for gp_external_max_segments and number of gpfdist processes.

gpfdist is installed in $GPHOME/bin on Greenplum master and segment servers/hosts.

- Starting and stopping gpfdist:
  - ° To start gpfdist:

```
$ gpfdist -d /var/load_files -p 8081 -l /home/gpadmin/log &
```

For multiple gpfdist instances on the same ETL host (refer figure on page 13), use a different base directory and port for each instance. For example:

```
$ gpfdist -d /var/load_files1 -p 8081 -l /home/gpadmin/log1 &
$ gpfdist -d /var/load_files2 -p 8082 -l /home/gpadmin/log2 &
```

  - ° To stop gpfdist when it is running in the background:

First find its process id:

```
$ ps -ef | grep gpfdist
```

Then kill the process, for example (where 3456 is the process ID in this example):

```
$ kill xxxx
```

gpload

The gpload data loading utility is used to load data into Greenplum's external table in parallel. gpload uses YAML formatted control file that has the following commands/scripts to load data into the target database:

- Invoke the Greenplum parallel file server program (gpfdist)
- Create an external table definition based on the source data defined
- Load the source data into the target table in the database according to gpload mode (insert, update, or merge)

It is important to note that with GPLOAD we have to deal with YAML, which is not simple and requires skill. But, as it acts as a wrapper simplifying multiple implementations into one, we can have parallel file-based external table setup with configuration of the data format, external table definition, and gpfdist or gpfdists setup in a single configuration file. It executes SQL against the external table. The external temporary external table is dropped once the load gets completed.

For example, `test.yml`:

```
%YAML 1.1
---
//Greenplum database connection configurations
VERSION: 1.0.0.1
DATABASE: master
USER: master
PASSWORD: master
HOST: master
PORT: 5432
GPLOAD:
//Gpfdist configurations
   INPUT:
     - SOURCE:
       LOCAL_HOSTNAME:
         - master
       PORT: 8082
       FILE:
         - /home/ master /SAMPLE.csv
//External table configurations
       - COLUMNS:
         - column1: numeric
         - column2: text
       - FORMAT: csv
       - DELIMITER: ","
       - ESCAPE: '/'
       - NULL_AS: '/N'
       - QUOTE: '"'
       - ENCODING: 'utf8'
       - ERROR_LIMIT: 5
       - ERROR_TABLE: test.load_error
   OUTPUT:
     - TABLE: test.sample
     - MODE: INSERT
   PRELOAD:
```

The result is as shown:

```
[master@ master mdp]$ gpload -f test.yml
2013-08-03 14:52:19|INFO|gpload session started 2013-05-03 14:52:19
2013-08-03 14:52:19|INFO|started gpfdist -p 8082 -P 8083 -f
  "/home/master/SAMPLE.csv" -t 30
2013-08-03 14:52:19|INFO|running time: 0.25 seconds
2013-08-03 14:52:19|INFO|rows Inserted          = 4
2013-08-03 14:52:19|INFO|rows Updated           = 0
2013-08-03 14:52:19|INFO|data formatting errors = 0
2013-08-03 14:52:19|INFO|gpload succeeded
```

The `gpload` program processes the control file document in order and uses indentation to demarcate the hierarchy. White spaces and tabs usage are restricted.

Hadoop (HD) data loading options

We will now look at ways to load data into Hadoop. To handle unstructured data processing and analytics, Greenplum provides a commercial Hadoop distribution with some proprietary integration pieces built to work with Greenplum Database, Chorus, and Command Center.

Sqoop 2

In this section, we will explore an option for data loading and unloading requirements for Hadoop with Sqoop API. Sqoop is a framework that ships with Hadoop and forms a part of Hadoop ecosystem as listed in *Chapter 2*, *Greenplum Unified Analytics Platform (UAP)*. This section is not meant to be a tutorial for Sqoop, but is intended to introduce the readers to this concept.

Data can be loaded independently into Hadoop using Sqoop API. As databases are not vastly accessible by Hadoop, Apache Hadoop was added to Hadoop ecosystem for efficiently transferring bulk data between Hadoop and structured databases. Sqoop is used for loading or unloading data from database/data warehouse, and NOSQL stores into HDFS. It comes with a connector-based architecture, where it can support multiple plugins. Have a look at the following figure:

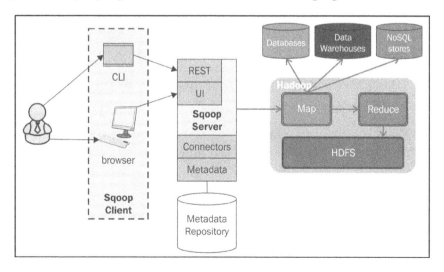

The following example demonstrates a `sqoop` command to import data from a data store using JDBC connector into Hive tables (more on Hive is covered in the next sections of this chapter).

```
sqoop import \
--connect jdbc:<<pjdbc connectors>> \
--username <<name>> \
--password <<password>> \
--table <<hive-table-name>> \
--hive-import
```

The advantage with Sqoop is that, it automatically creates the metadata for the Hive table. In the case where the Hive table does not exist, it creates the same.

To learn more on Apache Sqoop refer `http://sqoop.apache.org/docs/1.99.2/BuildingSqoop2.html`.

Greenplum BulkLoader for Hadoop

As a part of the HD distribution, Greenplum ships data loader components to help bulk load large volumes of data into HDFS. This section again introduces readers to bulk loader options in Greenplum for HD but is not intended to serve as a tutorial.

Greenplum Data Loader is a batch data-loading tool that leverages the GPHD MapReduce framework. Greenplum Data Loader manages a cluster of machines that support multijob/multiuser, parallel data loading, and optimizes disk/network bandwidth for best possible throughput.

The following are the functions:

- Deployment of code
- Partitioning of data into chunks
- Splitting jobs into multiple tasks
- Scheduling the tasks, taking into account data locality, and network topology
- Handling any job failures

Greenplum Data Loader can dynamically scale the execution of data loading tasks to maximize the system resource. It can linearly scale out to multiple disks or multiple machines depending on the cluster setup.

Additionally, Greenplum Data Loader component supports a wide variety of source data store/access protocols—HDFS, local FS (DAS), NFS, FTP, and HTTPS. It internally uses master/slave architecture and can be managed through both CLI and GUI.

Bulk loader components are listed in the following table:

Component	Summary
BulkLoader manager	An administrative GUI for managing data load processing. Provides REST interfaces to integrate with any other external clients.
BulkLoader scheduler	This is a job scheduling service to help schedule loading jobs.
BulkLoader CLI	This is a command-line interface to run loading jobs.

The Greenplum Data Loader cluster copies data from the source data store to the destination cluster. The cluster is composed of three types of logical nodes.

 The three nodes are master node, slave node and BulkLoader CLI node. Any existing MapReduce and HDFS deployment can be leveraged.

The following figure depicts various components in Hadoop HDFS and the BulkLoader components.

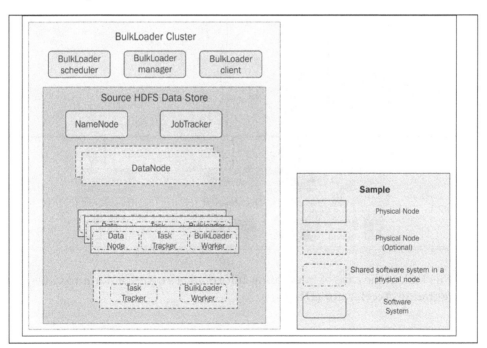

Using external ETL to load data into Greenplum

All the Greenplum utilities discussed earlier have some limitations in terms of what data source formats they can support; and we have seen that they are typically the file formats such as TXT, XML, CSV, and other custom formats.

As a further step to supporting any other data source formats, Greenplum can be integrated with an external data integration tool such as Informatica, Pentaho, Talend, and others. As a part of Data Integration Accelerator Module, Greenplum provides integration end points with these ETL to facilitate high-speed parallel data loading into the Greenplum Database. The following figure depicts the flow of how an external ETL server can load data directly into the segment servers to achieve high throughput.

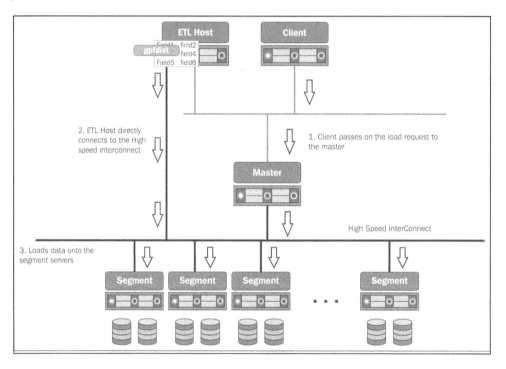

Now, let us look at the case of integrating Informatica PowerCenter into Greenplum **Data Integration Accelerator (DIA)**.

Informatica has PWX connectors for Greenplum that facilitate high-speed parallel data loading. The Greenplum Database is designed to load large volumes of data quickly with few jobs running in parallel. In order to take advantage of Greenplum's capabilities, such large volume loads through Informatica should use PWX for Greenplum. PWX for Greenplum utilizes the Greenplum load utilities `gpload/ gpfdist` that takes advantage of the database's massively parallel, shared nothing architecture.

We can use Informatica PWX Connector for Greenplum with Greenplum DIA. The segment servers of Greenplum connect directly to the external files served via `gpfdist`. The load bypasses the master server in this case. Segment servers are then loaded in parallel. The external tables point to the streamed files on the ETL host.

The loader utilities allow for loading of data to a single table. If a PowerCenter mapping has multiple Greenplum targets, PWX for Greenplum starts a separate loader instance for each target. Each loader instance will have a separate connection to Greenplum. The total number of Greenplum connections used is the number of Greenplum targets in the mapping multiplied by the number of partitions configured in the session. For mappings with many targets and/or many partitions, the number of Greenplum connections used may not be allowed by the database, or may cause out of memory issues on the Greenplum segments. In that case consider staging the data to a Greenplum staging table and using follow-on processing to load from there to the target tables. Refer the following section on ETLT for more details on this. Please refer to the Greenplum documentation for information on database connections.

Following is the workflow between Informatica and Greenplum servers:

- PWX for Greenplum starts a `gpload` process providing it a configuration file for the work to be done. It also creates a named pipe to pass data to `gpfdist`.
- `gpload` kicks off a `gpfdist` process and `gpfdist` process provides data to Greenplum segments.
- `gpload` communicates with Greenplum Database and sets up the load.
- The Greenplum master communicates with the Greenplum segment servers and instructs them to connect back to the `gpfdist` process to start pulling in data.
- The Greenplum segment servers connect with `gpfdist` and request the data.
- PWX for Greenplum writes data to the named pipe, `gpfdist` reads it from the named pipe, and the Greenplum segment servers pull data in directly from `gpfdist`.

The DIA servers, combined with the massively parallel processing databases in the DCA, are perfectly configured to be used as nodes in a PowerCenter grid. The scalability nature of the DIA allows you to add power and performance to your Informatica grid when more performance is needed for your data integration projects. In this case where Informatica is installed within DIA, the data load leverages the high-speed interconnect to load data.

Extraction, Load, and Transformation (ELT) and Extraction, Transformation, Load, and Transformation (ETLT)

ELT and ETLT are highly performing approaches when working with Informatica and Greenplum. Informatica can be used for complex parsing of source data and for transformation that can be achieved without looking up large numbers of records against large Greenplum tables. The data can be loaded to Greenplum staging tables using PWX for Greenplum. Any remaining transformation logic in Greenplum can be achieved in one of the following ways:

- Greenplum scripts
- Informatica push-down optimization
- Metadata driven Greenplum scripting

The connector can be integrated into Workflow Manager of PowerCenter as a target writer.

Greenplum target configuration

Use the following target configuration for all PWX for Greenplum targets. This will ensure that certain characters are escaped correctly, and prevent data loss and/or code page conversion errors.

```
Format - CSV
Delimiter - |
Escape - \
Skip Escaping - Unchecked
Null As -\N
Quote - "
Encoding - WIN1252
```

Sourcing large volumes of data from Greenplum

One way to communicate with Greenplum is to configure ODBC connection for Greenplum in Informatica, and this can prove to be inefficient in case of large volumes; another way is to use the File-based Writable External Table feature in Greenplum. Details on using external tables are discussed earlier in this chapter. Also, refer the Greenplum Admin Guide for more information on this feature.

The following steps are required to integrate Greenplum File-based Writable External Tables and Informatica:

1. Using a shell script (perhaps executed from a command task), perform the following steps:

    1. Create an empty directory on the Informatica server, for example, `mkdir /path/to/new/dir`.

    2. Start `gpfdist` on an available port against that directory, for example, `gpfdist -d /path/to/new/dir -p 8081 -l /path/to/log/dir/gpfdist.log`.

    3. Create a named pipe in the directory, for example, `mkfifo /path/to/new/dir/data.fifo`.

2. Execute SQL commands against the Greenplum database (perhaps in simple mappings using a SQLT):

    1. First create a writable external table, for example, `gpinfa.unload_us_person (like gpinfa.us_person)`.

    2. The location is `gpfdist://<InformaticaServer>:8081/us_person1.out`.

    3. The format is `'TEXT' (DELIMITER ',')`.

    4. It is distributed by `person_id`.

    5. Insert records from the table to be sourced into the writable external table, for example, insert into `gpinfa.unload_us_person select * from gpinfa.us_person`.

3. At this point Greenplum will start sending data to the `gpfdist` process on the Informatica server, which in turn will write the data to the named pipe. This process will be blocked and will not complete until another process reads from the named pipe. At this point, the Informatica session can begin reading the data from the named pipe and processing it as desired.

4. Once the session has been completed, the preceding insert statement will complete. Additional SQL commands can be executed to drop the file-based writable external table. Again this could perhaps be done using a mapping that executes after the main load and uses a SQLT to execute the SQL, for example, drop external table `gpinfa.unload_us_person`.

5. Final cleanup on the file system can be done using command tasks:

    1. Delete the named pipe, for example, `rm /path/to/new/dir/data.fifo`.

    2. Stop `gpfdist`. There are many ways to do this, but an easy way is to pass part or all of the command executed earlier to the `pkill` command, for example, pkill -f -u <user> " gpfdist -d /path/to/new/dir -p 8081 -l /path/to/log/dir/gpfdist.log "

    3. Remove the directory that was created, e.g. rmdir /path/to/new/dir

Here is a PowerCenter workflow that illustrates how these steps could be implemented in PowerCenter.

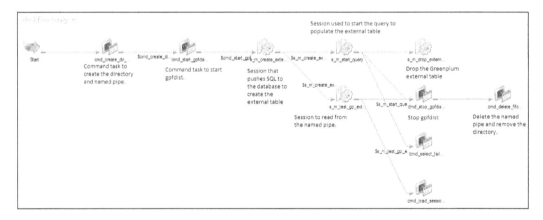

Unsupported Greenplum data types

PowerExchange for Greenplum does not support the following Greenplum data types:

- `bigserial`
- `bytea`
- `line`
- `serial`
- `time with time zone`
- `timestamp with time zone`

When you import a Greenplum table that contains columns with unsupported data types, the designer imports the columns. When you run a session, the results are unpredictable, and can include session failures. The gpload utility also fails and logs an error in the gpload log file.

Push Down Optimization (PDO)

In standard configuration all PowerCenter mapping logic gets implemented as a PowerCenter process running on the EIP servers. In situations where data is read from a database, some transformation logic is applied, and then the data is loaded back to the same database, it can make more sense to have the database do the transformation work internally. Informatica has a **Push Down Optimization (PDO)** feature that enables this. PDO allows developers to build mapping logic in the standard PowerCenter GUI development environment that is pushed to the database as SQL at execution time. It gives the performance benefit of executing in the database and the development and maintenance benefits of working in the PowerCenter client.

For simple Greenplum to Greenplum data loads, consider using PDO over ODBC. Note that not all PowerCenter logic can be pushed down to the database, so it will be important to verify which business logic can be implemented successfully through PDO. A limited number of transformations can be implemented using PDO over ODBC.

Greenplum table distribution and partitioning

In the following section, we will define table distribution in Greenplum context and detail the other related aspects of distribution, like data skew.

Distribution

Greenplum is a massive parallel processing data store, and data is distributed across segments as per the definition of the distribution strategy.

Every table in Greenplum has a data distribution method, the DISTRIBUTED BY clause helps define the distribution strategy. We need to ensure that there is no data skew introduced on any of the segment hosts as a result of the distribution key defined.

There are two methods of distributing table data across segment hosts:

- **Column oriented/Hash distribution**: This is a distribution mechanism that considers a column or a combination of columns to distribute data across segments:

```
DISTRIBUTED BY (column name(s))
```

- **Random distribution**: In this distribution mechanism data would be distributed across the segment servers in a round robin fashion. In this approach there wouldn't be any data skew on the segments. For any table that uses a random distribution, either redistribution or broadcast operation will be required to perform a table join. There are performance implications when performing a redistribution or broadcast of very large tables. Random distribution should be used for small tables and when a Hash distribution method is not feasible due to significant data skew:

```
DISTRIBUTED RANDOMLY
```

Distribution key can be modified at any point of time. In case the table has any unique key, that key needs to be considered in the distributed key. User-defined data types cannot be included into distributed key. Every table has a default distribution strategy and we should not be using that as it may introduce skew. In Hash distributions, a lot of care needs to be taken to ensure there is no data skew seen. The following are few important considerations while defining Hash distribution keys:

- Use keys with unique values and high cardinality to distribute the data evenly across all segment instances.
- Avoid Boolean keys like T/F, Y/N, or 1/0.
- With data skew problem solved, ensure there wouldn't be computational skew. Let us take an example where the distribution key had a DATE column and the data is always evenly distributed; and in case where there are queries to get and process data for a particular month, it could happen that a particular segment will end up serving all the requests, thus resulting in computational skew.

Distribution key definition should depend on the data schema structure and most common querying patterns. Commonly used joined tables should use same data types for distribution keys. One important note that database designers should consider is that, every time a query is fired that might involve joining data between segment server, Greenplum would internally do a co-location exercise or redistribution motion to respond to the query request, that would be destroyed post communicating the results to the client.

The co-location or redistribution motion is all about the process, where to perform a local join matching rows must be located together on the same segment instance and in absence of which a dynamic redistribution of the needed rows from one of the tables to another segment instance will be performed. This might prove to be expensive for the table with large volumes of data and might just work fine for smaller tables.

In some cases a broadcast motion will be performed rather than a redistribute motion. In a broadcast motion, every segment instance performs a broadcast or sends its own individual rows to all other segment instances. This will result in every segment instance having its own complete and local copy of the entire table. A broadcast motion may not be as optimal as a redistribute motion. Therefore, the optimizer typically selects a broadcast motion only for very small tables. A broadcast motion is not acceptable for large tables.

Following is the syntax for defining distribution strategy for a table in Greenplum:

```
CREATE TABLE tablename (
column_name1 data_type   NOT NULL,
column_name2 data_type   NOT NULL,
Column_name3 data_type   NOT NULL ...)
[DISTRIBUTE BY (column_name)] à Hash algorithm
[DISTRIBUTED RANDOMLY] à Round-robin algorithm
```

Data skew and performance

In an MPP shared nothing environment, overall response time for a query is measured by the completion time for all segments. If the data is skewed, the segments with more data will have a longer completion time. The optimal goal is that each segment should have a comparable number of rows and perform approximately the same amount of processing. Have a look at the following figure:

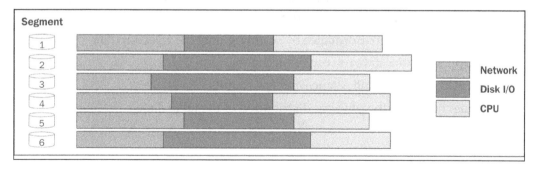

Optimizing the broadcast or redistribution motion for data co-location

A broadcast motion is usually not as optimal as a redistribute motion for very large tables. The gp_segments_for_planner configuration should be used to optimize the impact due to broadcast or redistribution operation.

By default, this configuration parameter takes value 0. gp_segments_for_planner sets the number of primary segment instances for the planner to assume in its cost and size estimates.

- If gp_segments_for_planner is set to 0, the value used is the actual number of primary segments. This variable affects the planner's estimates of the number of rows handled by each sending and receiving process in motion operators.

- Increasing the number of primary segments will increase the cost of the motion, hence favoring a redistribute motion over a broadcast motion.

- For example, setting gp_segments_for_planner = 100000 tells the planner that there are 100,000 segments.

Partitioning

Table partitioning is used to logically divide large tables to improve performance and facilitate data warehouse maintenance tasks. The primary goal of table partitioning is to eliminate scanning partitions that contain data that is not needed to satisfy a query. Consider table partitioning on large tables that can be divided into somewhat equal parts based on a defining criterion and the defining criteria is used in query predicates (WHERE clause). Following are the important features of table partitioning:

- Addresses the problem of supporting very large tables (such as fact tables) by dividing them into smaller and more manageable pieces

- Improves query performance by scanning only the relevant data

- Supports easier data roll out for archiving

- Works with table inheritance and constraints

- Does not affect the physical distribution of the table data

Partitioning can be range or list based. We can define a date range, numeric range, or a list. The following is an example of range partitioning:

```
CREATE TABLE sales (id int, date date, amt decimal(10,2))
  DISTRIBUTED BY (id)
PARTITIONED BY RANGE (date)
(PARTITION Jan13 START (date '2013-01-01') INCLUSIVE,
PARTITION Feb13 START (date '2013-02-01') INCLUSIVE,
PARTITION Mar13 START (date '2013-03-01') INCLUSIVE,
...
PARTITION Dec13 START (date '2013-12-01') INCLUSIVE
END (date '2014-01-01') EXCLUSIVE );
```

The following is an example of list partitioning:

```
CREATE TABLE ranking (id int, rank int, gender char(1), count int)
  DISTRIBUTED BY (id)
PARTITIONED BY LIST (gender)
(PARTITION women VALUES ('F'),
PARTITION men VALUES ('M')
DEFAULT PARTITION other);
```

Partition elimination is a process in which irrelevant data is filtered out, thus reducing table scans. This process can occur either as a part of the query plan or during the query execution time.

The following is an example of dynamic partition elimination:

- Building partition table using list:

```
CREATE TABLE performance_quarter (LIKE another_table)
DISTRIBUTED BY (id)
PARTITION BY LIST (quartered)
(PARTITION first_quarter VALUES(1),
PARTITION second_quarter VALUES(2),
PARTITION third_quarter VALUES(3),
PARTITION fourth_quarter VALUES(4));
```

- Dynamic partition elimination while querying the fact:

```
SELECT * FORM performance_quarter, dimquarter WHERE
  dimquarter.description like 'Quarter1%' AND
    performance_quarter.id = dimquarter.quarterid
```

The primary goal of table partitioning is to eliminate scanning partitions that contain data that is not needed to satisfy a query. Following are some important guidelines to follow while defining table partitions:

- Partitioning should be used for very large tables, such as fact tables, to improve query performance. For smaller tables, unless there is a significant performance benefits that overweigh the administrative overhead, do not go for partitioning.

- The partitioning strategy should facilitate dividing data into somewhat equal parts based on a defining criteria and the defining criteria is used in query predicates (WHERE clause). If the query access pattern (SELECT....WHERE) does not match the partitioning definition, the benefit of partition elimination cannot be maximized.

- When defining partitioning criteria, it is important to not have overlapping ranges if using range partitioning, and to ensure list values are unique if using list partitioning.

- Use the pg_partitions view to get information on the partition design.

- To partition an existing table, you must recreate and reload the table as a partitioned table.

Querying Greenplum Database and HD

In the first section of this document, we have seen various options to load data (both structured and unstructured) into Greenplum environment in a parallel mode. In this section, we will focus on learning how to query data from Greenplum Database and HD environments. Also, we will explore interfaces that help integrate data between Greenplum Database and HD and leverage the benefit of holding one single copy of the data.

Querying Greenplum Database

Greenplum Database is built over PostgreSQL and supports all standard SQL and PL/SQL operations. Additionally, because of the distributed nature, there are few new options that are built for scaled performance over the data cluster.

Let us now look at how Greenplum executes queries across data from all the segments. Internally, it implements scatter/gather mechanism that is unique to Greenplum.

When working with Greenplum, we issue queries to the database similar to any other database. In the context of Greenplum, the internal implementation however varies:

- The master host receives, parses, and optimizes the query, creates a parallel query plan, and dispatches the same plan to all the segments for execution.

- Each segment is responsible for executing local database operations on its own set of data. The segments are scanned in parallel.

 Once the query is executed, the results are returned to the master, which in turn returns the results to the client. Optimal distribution and partitioning strategy is key to the query performance.

Analyzing and optimizing queries

The ANALYZE function

It is very critical to get statistics to realize good query plans that would give good results. The ANALYZE operation requires only a read lock on the table and can possibly run in parallel.

For INSERT, UPDATE, DELETE, and CREATE INDEX operations, always run ANALYZE after running the queries. We should use gp_autostats_on_change_threshold in conjunction with gp_autostats_mode to auto analyze during these operations.

Following is the syntax for the ANALYZE command:

```
ANALYZE [table  [ (column  [, ...] ) ]]
```

ANALYZE by default analyzes all tables and all columns unless specified. The statistics for the following scenarios would be useful:

- The JOIN condition
- The WHERE clause
- The SORT clause
- The GROUP BY or HAVING clause

The EXPLAIN function

The EXPLAIN function displays the query execution plan for the query. Every node represents a single operation and it reads plans from bottom-up as each node feeds rows into the nodes directly above it. The bottom nodes of a plan are usually sequential table scan operations. The topmost plan nodes are usually the motion nodes (redistribute, explicit redistribute, broadcast, or gather motions). These are the operations responsible for moving rows between the segment instances during query processing.

The EXPLAIN ANALYZE function is run on queries to identify any areas where the query performance can be improved. This function always executes the query.

The following syntax should be used to run EXPLAIN ANALYZE; we would need to use the EXPLAIN ANALYZE explicitly in a transaction:

```
BEGIN; EXPLAIN ANALYZE ...; ROLLBACK;
```

Dynamic Pipelining in Greenplum

Dynamic Pipelining framework enables parallel data flow both during distribution and querying. Following are the key aspects of this feature:

- Combines high-speed UDP interconnect and a runtime execution environment for big data workloads
- Data from upstream components in the dynamic pipeline are transmitted to downstream components through UDP interconnect
- Enables queries to run without materializing intermediate contents to disk

The following figure explains the function of this feature:

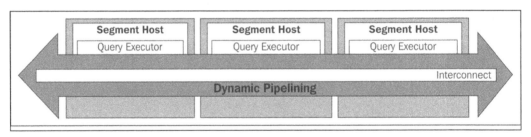

Querying HDFS

Hadoop ecosystem provides Pig and Hive frameworks to query data from HDFS. In the latest versions of HD under Pivotal endeavor, HAWQ framework (SQL-like querying interface for HD) is being released. We will not be covering HAWQ in this book.

Let's take a quick look at what Pig and Hive frameworks are all about and understand how HDFS data can be queried using some examples.

Hive

In this section, we will focus on understanding how to use Hive to access data stored in HDFS. The following figure depicts Hive architecture.

Hive has the following dependencies to run successfully:

- Java 6
- Hadoop framework and Hadoop home directory configured

Hive internally runs in a MapReduce mode for efficiency. Hive is an SQL-like interface that can query data on HDFS.

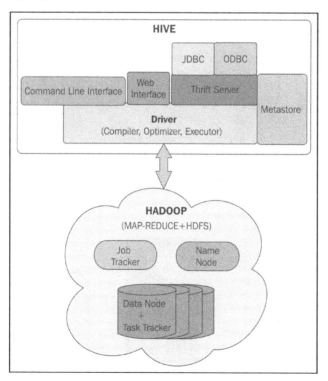

For example:

1. Passing CSV data onto HDFS using the following commands:

    ```
    $ hadoop fs -mkdir input
    $ hadoop fs -put /Users/Test/Data/Source/Books.csv input
    ```

2. Run Hive from command line to create a data structure around the
    imported data:

    ```
    $ hive
    hive> CREATE TABLE IF NOT EXISTS BOOKSDATA
        >    (ISBN STRING,
        >    BookTitle STRING,
        >    BookAuthor STRING,
        >    YearOfPublication STRING,
        >    Publisher STRING,
        >    ImageURLS STRING,
        >    ImageURLM STRING,
        >    ImageURLL STRING)
        > COMMENT 'BX-Books Table'
        > ROW FORMAT DELIMITED
        > FIELDS TERMINATED BY ';'
        > STORED AS TEXTFILE;
    OK
    Time taken: 0.086 seconds
    ```

3. Query data from the structure created above:

    ```
    hive> LOAD DATA INPATH '/user/Test/data/source/Books.csv'
      OVERWRITE INTO TABLE BOOKSDATA ;
    Loading data to table default.booksdata
    Deleted hdfs://localhost:9000/user/hive/warehouse/bxdataset
    OK
    Time taken: 0.192 seconds

    hive> select yearofpublication, count(booktitle) from
      booksdata group by yearofpublication;
    ```

4. Result of the preceding query:

Pig

The purpose of Pig is similar to Hive with the only difference being that Hive is more SQL-like interface and is usually used by developers who are familiar and comfortable with SQL. For those from a non-SQL background, Pig is an option, where developers can write Java code that runs as a MapReduce function to query data on HDFS.

Pig supports many data types and developers can create custom functions in Java, Python, and JavaScript. Its simple interface eases writing complex joins and other functions.

Pig can be executed in local or MapReduce mode shown as follows:

```
$ pig -x local  grunt>
OR
$ pig
  [main] INFO  org.apache.pig.Main - Apache Pig version 0.10.0
  (r1328203) compiled Apr 19 2013, 22:54:12
  [main] INFO  org.apache.pig.Main - Logging error messages to:
  /Users/test/pig_1351858332488.log
  [main] INFO
    org.apache.pig.backend.hadoop.executionengine.HExecutionEngine
      - Connecting to hadoop file system at: hdfs://localhost:9000
  main] INFO
    org.apache.pig.backend.hadoop.executionengine.HExecutionEngine
      - Connecting to map-reduce job tracker at: localhost:9001
  grunt>
```

For example:

```
grunt> CountByYear = FOREACH GroupByYear
>> GENERATE
  CONCAT((chararray)$0,CONCAT(':',(chararray)COUNT($1)));
2012-11-05 01:09:11,996 [main] WARN  org.apache.pig.PigServer -
  Encountered Warning IMPLICIT_CAST_TO_DOUBLE 1 time(s).
grunt> STORE CountByYear >> INTO
  '/user/work/output/pig_output_bookx' USING PigStorage('t');
```

Data communication between Greenplum Database and Hadoop (using external tables)

Greenplum supports exchanging HDFS data with Greenplum Database as external tables, allowing for the reading from and writing to the HDFS directly from the Greenplum Database, with the HDFS supporting full SQL syntax.

This combination leverages the full parallelism of the Greenplum Database and the HDFS, utilizing the resource of all Greenplum segments when reading and writing data with the HDFS.

Data is read into the Greenplum Database as an external table directly from the HDFS DataNode, and it is written out from the Greenplum Database segment servers to the HDFS. This relies on the HDFS to distribute data load evenly across the DataNodes.

Following are the steps to read data from Hadoop HDFS into Greenplum Database:

1. Greenplum initiates read request from Greenplum with Hadoop NameNode having access to the required file blocks.

2. Hadoop NameNode sends instruction to DataNode to provide file blocks to Greenplum thus addressing the read request.

Following are the steps to write data to Hadoop HDFS from Greenplum Database:

1. Greenplum (client) initiates write request with Hadoop NameNode having access to the required file blocks.

2. Hadoop NameNode sends instruction to DataNode to update the file blocks into the file including the instruction for any data replication.

 In the newer versions of UAP, there are new integration frameworks being built, like HAWQ, that provide SQL-like querying capabilities over HD and can query Greenplum Database and HD combined to provide the client with a single shot view on data across Greenplum Database and HD.

Data Computing Appliance (DCA)

In *Chapter 2, Greenplum Unified Analytics Platform (UAP)*, we were introduced to **Data Computing Appliance (DCA)** of Greenplum, In this section we will take a dive deep into the configuration options in DCA.

There are four important layers in DCA. The following table explains the functions for each layer:

Layer	Description
Compute	Currently, the latest intel processor for excellent compute node performance
Storage	High-density RAID protected disks
Database	Greenplum Database incorporating MPP
Network	Dual 10Gig Ethernet switches for high-speed data communication between nodes

The following table provides the hardware details on the DCA UAP edition modules. Notably, now there are five modules to deploy from:

- Greenplum Database compute, four 2RU servers per module
- Greenplum Database standard, four 2RU servers per module
- GPHD, four 2RU servers per module
- GPHD—compute, two 1RU servers per module, and for computation only
- GP DIA, two 1RU servers per module

 This may be changing with the next DCA release.

Module	Figure	Size	Hardware
Greenplum Database Compute Module		9TB Data (uncompressed)	Four 2U servers per module, each server contains: • Two Sandy Bridge sockets/16 cores • 64 GB memory • 24 x 300 GB SAS 10K drives
Greenplum Database Standard Module		27.5TB Data (uncompressed)	Four 2U servers per module, each server contains: • Two sandy bridge sockets/16 cores • 64 GB memory • 24 x 900 GB SAS 10K drives
HD Module		36TB Data (3 copies, uncompressed)	Four 2U servers per module, each server contains: • Two sandy bridge sockets/16 cores • 64 GB memory • 12 x 3 TB SATA 7.2K drives
HD Compute Module		Compute-only	Two 1U servers, each server contains: • Two sandy bridge sockets/16 cores • 64 GB memory
DIA Module		2.7TB Data	Two 1U servers, each server contains: • Two sandy bridge sockets/16 cores • 64 GB memory • 6 x 300 GB SAS 10K drives

Storage design, disk protection, and fault tolerance

In this section let us explore storage configurations used for master and segment servers in Greenplum. They both use RAID 5 for redundancy and disk protection.

Master server RAID configurations

In DCA, each master server has six disks. They are laid out for RAID 5 (4+1) configuration with one hot backup. This configuration helps with additional fault tolerance on the master servers. The following table explains the RAID configurations for Master server:

RAID group	Physical disks	Virtual disks	Function	File system	Capacity
RAID group 1	5	Virtual disk 1	ROOT	Ext3	48 GB
		Virtual disk 2	SWAP	SWAP	48 GB
		Virtual disk 3	DATA	XFS	2.09 TB
Hot spare	1	None	Hot spare		

The following figure depicts the master server RAID configurations as per the listing in the preceding table:

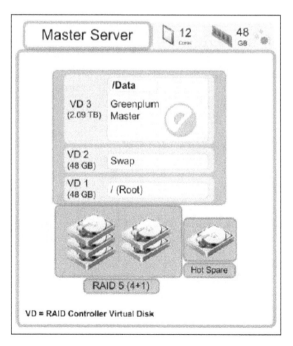

Segment server RAID configurations

Each segment server in DCA has 12 disks that have two RAID groups of RAID 5 (5+1) attached. DCA maximizes the I/O performance by using the following RAID controller policies:

- Disabled disk cache policy
- Write policy for write back
- Read policy for adaptive read ahead

The segment instances are equally spread across two file systems: /data1 and /data2. The table below details the RAID configurations for the segment servers.

RAID group	Physical disks	Virtual disks	Function	File system	Capacity
RAID group 1	6	Virtual disk 1	ROOT	Ext3	48 GB
		Virtual disk 2	DATA1	XFS	2.68 TB
RAID group 2	6	Virtual disk 1	ROOT	Ext3	48 GB
		Virtual disk 2	DATA2	XFS	2.68 TB

The next image demonstrates the RAID configurations for the segment servers and is a depiction of the data in the table above.

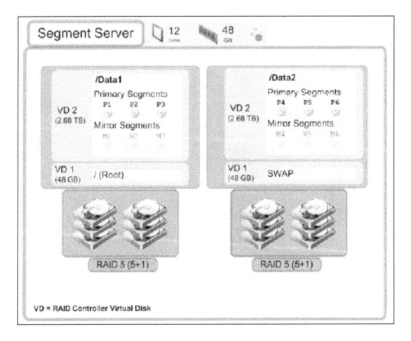

Monitoring DCA

Greenplum Command Center helps administrators and developers measure the query and system performance metrics for DCA. It integrates HD, database, and chorus components and provides a single shot view into the health of the system.

To monitor the performance of the appliance, there are performance agents that run on the master and the segment servers. The agents collect performance data on query execution and system utilization and send it to dedicated command center database (gpperfmon) at regular intervals. This database is located on the master server and contains three types of tables: now, history, and tail. Master agent polls all segment agents for system metrics and other data at a configurable interval and stores it in flat files and periodically commits the data to the database. Greenplum Database installation includes setup scripts to install the Command Center database. Now tables store data on current system metrics such as active queries, history tables store data on historical metrics, and tail tables are for data in transition. Tail tables are for internal use only. Now and tail data are stored as text files on the master host file system and accessed by the Command Center database via external tables. The history tables are regular database tables.

The following functions can be executed from the Command Center:

- **Database administration**: Ability to stop/start the database and ability to recover/rebalance segments
- **Interactive view of system metrics**: Real-time and historic (configurable by time)
- **Database query monitoring**: Ability to view, search, or cancel queries in the system, and ability to view the query plan
- **Database workload**: Ability to configure resource queues and ability to prioritize users

Have a look at the following screenshot:

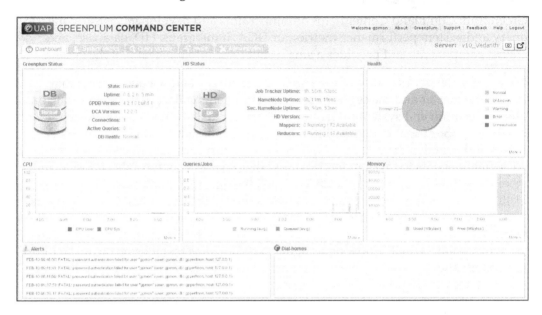

Optionally, Command Center may be installed on a web server on the master host. Command Center can be enabled or disabled using the gp_enable_gpperfmon server configuration parameter. $MASTER_DATA_DIRECTORY/gpperfmon/conf/ gpperfmon.conf stores configuration parameters for the Command Center agents. For configuration changes to take effect, the Pivotal DB must be restarted. For additional information refer to the Pivotal Command Center Administrators guide.

The following commands can be used to start/stop Command Center:

```
$ gpcmdr --start [instance_name]
$ gpcmdr --stop [instance_name]
```

There are other utilities in Greenplum Database that help monitor the health of Greenplum Database:

- **gpstate**: It displays information on which segments are down. It shows master and segment configuration information (hosts, data directories, and so on), the ports used by the system, and mapping of primary segments to their corresponding mirror segments.

- **gpcheckperf**: It helps identify hardware issues. This must have a trusted host setup between the hosts involved in the performance test. It calls to gpssh and gpscp, so these utilities must also be in our $PATH.

- **gpcheckperf**: It performs the following:

   ○ Disk I/O test

   ○ Memory bandwidth test (This utility uses the STREAM benchmark program to measure sustainable memory bandwidth (in MB/s) and network performance test (gpnetbench). This test is best used to validate if the switch fabric can tolerate a full-matrix workload. For additional information on gpstate and gpcheckperf refer to the Greenplum Database Utility guide.)

 gpcheckperf puts considerable strain on a system and should not be used on an active, production system.

Greenplum Database management

In this section, we will learn about a few in-built tools that help perform some Greenplum administration tasks as listed below:

- Starting and stopping Greenplum Database

- Adding new segment servers

- Loading data in parallel

- Parallel backup and restoring

- Managing recovery of failed segments, and so on

The following screenshot shows an object browser window in Greenplum's **pgAdminIII**, a client tool to manage database elements:

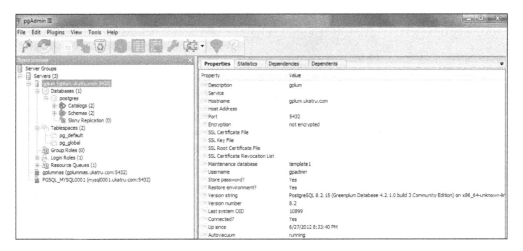

The next screenshot shows the query builder view of pgAdminIII, developers can use this interface to graphically build queries:

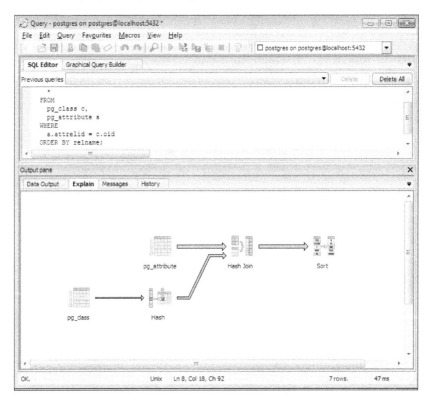

The following interface helps monitor the master and segment server status:

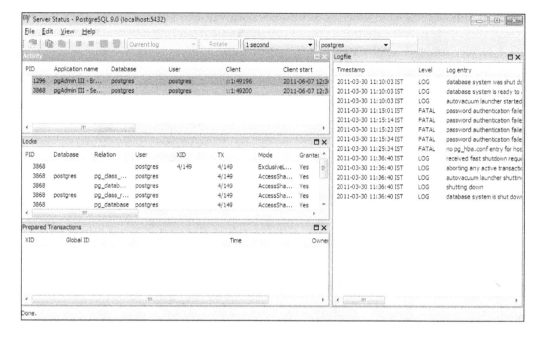

In-database analytics options (Greenplum-specific)

This section covers advanced SQL techniques for in-database analytics within Greenplum.

The following techniques will be discussed in detail:

- Windows functions
- User-defined functions and aggregates

Window functions

Window functions are a new class of functions introduced in Greenplum. The WINDOW clause is used to define a window that can be used in the OVER() expression of a window function such as rank or avg. For information on OLAP extensions and window functions refer to the Greenplum Database Reference guide. Window functions allow application developers to more easily compose complex OLAP queries using standard SQL commands. For example:

* Moving averages or sums can be calculated over various intervals.

* Aggregations and ranks can be reset as selected column values change.

* Complex ratios can be expressed in simple terms. Window functions can only be used in the SELECT list, between the SELECT and FROM keywords of a query.

Unlike aggregate functions, which return a result value for each group of rows, window functions return a result value for every row, but that value is calculated with respect to the rows in a particular window partition (grouping) or window frame (row position within the window).

What classifies a function as a window function is the use of an OVER clause. The OVER clause defines the window of data to which the function will be applied.

There are three characteristics of a window function:

* **zPartitions (groupings)**: A window function calculates the results for a row with respect to its partition

* **Ordering of rows within a window partition**: Some window functions such as RANK require ordering

* **Framing**: For ordered result sets, you can define a window frame that analyzes each row with respect to the rows directly above or below it

All window functions must have an OVER() clause. The window function specifies the window of data to which the function applies it defines:

* Window partitions using the PARTITION BY clause

* Ordering within a window partition using the ORDER BY clause

* Framing within a window partition (ROWS/RANGE clauses)

The PARTITION BY clause

The PARTITION BY clause performs the following functions:

- It can be used by all window functions. However, it is not a required clause. Windows that do not use the PARTITION BY clause present the entire result set as a single window partition.

- It organizes the result set into groupings based on the unique values of the specified expression or column.

- It allows the function to be applied to each partition independently.

The ORDER BY clause

The ORDER BY clause is used to order the resulting data set based on an expression or column. It is always allowed in windows functions and is required by some window functions, including RANK. The ORDER BY clause specifies ordering within a window partition.

The RANK function is a built-in function that calculates the rank of a row in an ordered group of values. Rows with equal values for the ranking criteria receive the same rank. The number of tied rows is added to the rank number to calculate the next rank value. In this case, ranks may not be consecutive numbers.

A moving or rolling window defines a set of rows within a window partition. When you define a window frame, the window function is computed with respect to the contents of this moving frame, rather than against the fixed content of the entire window partition. Window frames can be row-based, represented by the ROWS clause, or value-based, represented by a RANGE clause.

When the window frame is row-based, you define the number of rows offset from the current row. If the window frame is range-based, you define the bounds of the window frame in terms of data values offset from the value in the current row.

If you specify only a starting row for the window, the current row is used as the last row in the window.

The OVER (ORDER BY…) clause

Greenplum supports a variety of methods for developing functions, including:

- Query language support for functions developed in SQL

- Procedural language support for functions written in languages such as PL/pgSQL (which is a subset of PL/SQL), PL/TcL, Perl, Python, and R (a programming)

- Language for statistical computing and graphics

- Internal functions

- C-language functions

 The data scientist may need to create a function that could be used in the downstream analysis. Greenplum supports PL/pgSQL, PL/Perl, and PL/Python out of the box. Other languages can be added with the `createlang` utility.

Creating, modifying, and dropping functions

Functions that operate on tables must be created in the same schema. If you modify a table, we must have access to a schema.

- Create a function with the CREATE FUNCTION command. You must have CREATE access to the schema to create a function. A function can be created with or without parameters.

- Replace an existing function with the CREATE OR REPLACE FUNCTION command. This command either creates a function if one did not exist before, or replaces an existing function. If you are replacing an existing function, you must specify the same number of parameters and the same data types found in the original function. If not, you are actually creating a new function.

- Change a function with the ALTER FUNCTION command. You must own the function before you can modify it. If the function is to be created in another schema, you must have CREATE privilege on that schema.

- Drop or remove a function with the DROP FUNCTION command. Because you can have multiple functions with the same name but different number of parameters and/or parameter types, you must include the appropriate number of parameters and parameter types as part of the command. You must also be the owner of the function to remove the function from the schema.

User-defined aggregates

User-defined aggregates perform a single table scan and it keeps state. A state is a maximum of two numbers. In this example we create a user-defined aggregate that returns a maximum of two numbers.

CREATE AGGREGATE defines a new aggregate function. Some basic and commonly used aggregate functions such as count, min, max, sum, avg, and so on are already provided in the Greenplum Database.

If one defines new types or needs an aggregate function not already provided, then CREATE AGGREGATE can be used to provide the desired features.

An aggregate function is made from one, two, or three ordinary functions (mutually exclusive): a state transition function sfunc, an optional preliminary segment-level calculation function prefunc, and an optional final calculation function ffunc. These are used as follows:

- sfunc(internal-state, next-data-values) ---> next-internal-state
- prefunc(internal-state, internal-state) ---> next-internal-state
- ffunc(internal-state) ---> aggregate-value

In the preceding example we only have the sfunc.

To test this aggregate, you can try the following code:

```
CREATE TABLE x(a INT);
INSERT INTO x VALUES (1),(2),(3);
SELECT scube(a) FROM x;
Correct answer for reference:
SELECT sum(a*a*a) FROM x;
```

Aggregate function description:

```
array_agg(any element) Concatenates any element into an array.
   Example: SELECT array_agg(anyelement ORDER BY anyelement) FROM
     table;
string_agg(text) Concatenates text into a string. Example: SELECT
   string_agg(text ORDER BY text) FROM table;
string_agg(text, delimiter) Concatenates text into a string
   delimited by delimiter.
```

For example, SELECT string_agg(text, ',' ORDER BY text) FROM table;

The columns in an ORDER BY clause are not necessarily the same as the aggregated column, as shown in the following code that references a table named product with columns store_id, product_name, and quantity:

```
SELECT store_id, array_agg(product_name ORDER BY quantity desc) FROM
product GROUP BY store_id;
```

 There can only be one aggregated column. Multiple columns can be specified in the ORDER BY clause.

Using R with Greenplum

In *Chapter 3, Advanced Analytics – Paradigms, Tools, and Techniques*, we were introduced to R programming. R is a very powerful programming language that has many built-in libraries for running statistical and analytical calculation or modeling. In this section, we will learn how R functions can be integrated to work with data in Greenplum. There are many ways in which we can run R on the data from Greenplum and we will now discuss on the following two important approaches:

- R with standard DBI connector to Greenplum; in this case, R program connects to Postgres/Greenplum database, loads data into R client
- PL/R – procedural language for SQL calls to R functions

DBI Connector for R

From R program, we can access Postgres or Greenplum in the following way:

```
//Database connector code
require(TSP)
require(fields)
require(RPostgreSQL)
drv <- dbDriver("PostgreSQL")
conn <- dbConnect(drv, user="postgres", dbname="pgissc")
sql.str <- "select id, st_x(location) as x, st_y(location) as y,
location from stands;"
waypts <- dbGetQuery(conn, sql.str)
dist.matrix <- rdist.earth(waypts[,2:3], R=3949.0)
rtsp <- TSP(dist.matrix)
soln <- solve_TSP(rtsp)
tour <- as.vector(soln)
dbDisconnect(conn)
dbUnloadDriver(drv)
print(paste("tour.dist=", attributes(soln)$tour_length))
```

The output will be as follows:

```
[1] "tour.dist= 2804.58129355858"
```

PL/R

PL/R is a procedural language for R and is categorized under in-database processing option for Greenplum.

Following are the general installation steps for setting up PL/R. This needs to be done on every segment server.

```
tar -xzf plr-x.x.x.x.tar.gz
cd plr/
USE_PGXS=1 make
su -c "USE_PGXS=1 make install"
make installcheck
```

Following sample details the syntax for creating a PL/R function in Greenplum:

```
CREATE OR REPLACE FUNCTION func_name(arg-type1 [, arg-type2 ...])
RETURNS return-type AS $$
function body referencing arg1 [, arg2 ...]
$$ LANGUAGE ⊠plr⊠;
The above PL/R code is for an R function of the below syntax:func_name
<- function(arg1 [,arg2...]) {
function body referencing arg1 [,arg2 ...]
}
```

The following table represents the data type conversions between Postgres and R:

PostgreSQL Data Type	R Data Type
int2, int4	Integer
int8, oat4, oat8, cash, numeric	Numeric
Byte	Object
Everything else	Character
One-dimensional arrays	Multi-element R vectors
Two-dimensional arrays	R matrices
Three-dimensional arrays	Three-dimensional R arrays
Composite types	R data frames

The following code sample is an example for the PL/R version of the R code in the above section (DBI connector for R):

```
CREATE OR REPLACE FUNCTION tsp_tour_length() RETURNS float8 AS
$$
require(TSP)
require(fields)
require(RPostgreSQL)
drv <- dbDriver("PostgreSQL")
conn <- dbConnect(drv, user="postgres", dbname="pgissc")
sql.str <- "select id, st_x(location) as x, st_y(location) as y,
location from stands;"
waypts <- dbGetQuery(conn, sql.str)
dist.matrix <- rdist.earth(waypts[,2:3], R=3949.0)
rtsp <- TSP(dist.matrix)
soln <- solve_TSP(rtsp)
dbDisconnect(conn)
dbUnloadDriver(drv)
return(attributes(soln)$tour_length)
$$
LANGUAGE ⌷plr⌷ STRICT;

SELECT tsp_tour_length();
tsp_tour_length
-----------------
2804.58129355858
(1 row)
```

We can optionally auto load R functions in Postgres. There are special modules `plr_modules` that contain the R functions.

Using Weka with Greenplum

As saw seen in *Chapter 3, Advanced Analytics – Paradigms, Tools, and Techniques*, Weka is a Java-based analytics framework and an alternative to R. As it is a Java-based analytics API, it can connect to any database that supports or has a JDBC driver. Weka comes with a support to a wide range of database and in order to connect to Greenplum, we would need to use the `DatabaseUtils.props.postgresql` properties file and should be extracted to the HOME directory.

To connect to Postgres/Greenplum from Weka, configure the following properties in the `DatabaseUtils.props.postgresql` properties file:

```
jdbcDriver = org.postgresql.Driver
jdbcURL= jdbc:postgresql://<<domain>>:<<port>>/<<dbName>>
```

Weka has an API `InstanceQuery` that can be used in the following way to invoke a Postgres function or stored procedure from the command line:

```
java InstanceQuery -Q "SELECT * FROM stored_procedure_name()" -U <user>
-P <password>
```

Using MADlib with Greenplum

MAD stands for Magnetic, Agile, and Deep; and lib denotes a library of scalable, parallel, and advanced in-database functions. The following figure shows the architecture of MADlib. The MADlib version used in the following example is v1.1:

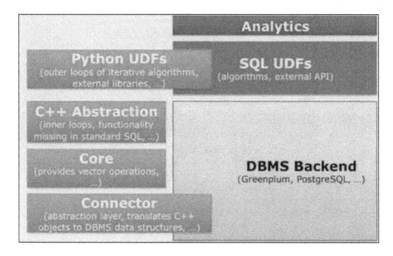

Greenplum Database extensions for MADlib would need to be installed on the segment servers on DCA.

```
$ pgxn install madlib
$ gppkg -i MADlib
```

The `gppkg` utility installs the MADlib extensions on all the Greenplum segment servers in parallel.

MADlib based in-database analytics is benchmarkedagainst PL/R and is found to be superior in terms of scalability and performance, and MADlib is a truly parallelized process as compared to PL/R.

Let us now look at an example of MADlib function implementation for linear regression.

As we have learned in *Chapter 3, Advanced Analytics – Paradigms, Tools, and Techniques,* linear regression is a statistical technique that helps fit data into a linear equation.

The MADlib prediction function that we would be using for this purpose is as shown:

```
linregr_predict(
  coeficient,
  col_ind
)
```

Following are the steps to implement and run MADlib functions in Greenplum:

1. Create the dataset for running regression function:

```
CREATE TABLE items (id INT, tax INT, quantity INT, price INT,
           size INT);
COPY items FROM STDIN WITH DELIMITER '|';
  59 |       2 |     1 |   500 |    770
 105 |       3 |     2 |   850 |   1410
   2 |       3 |     1 |   225 |   1060
  87 |       2 |     2 |   900 |   1300
 132 |       3 |     2 |  1330 |   1500
 135 |       2 |     1 |   905 |    820
 279 |       3 |   2.5 |  2600 |   2130
  68 |       2 |     1 |  1425 |   1170
 184 |       3 |     2 |  1600 |   1500
 368 |       4 |     2 |  2400 |   2790
 166 |       3 |     1 |   870 |   1030
 162 |       3 |     2 |  1186 |   1250
 310 |       3 |     2 |  1400 |   1760
 207 |       2 |     3 |  1480 |   1550
  65 |       3 |   1.5 |   650 |   1450
```

2. Build a regression model:

```
-- one regression model
SELECT madlib.linregr_train(
  'items', 'items_lr', 'price', 'array[1, tax]');


-- different output models
SELECT madlib.linregr_train(
  'items', 'items_lr_quantity', 'price', 'array[1, tax]',
    'quantity');
```

3. Analyze the results:

```
SELECT * from items_lr;
SELECT * FROM items_lr_quantity;
```

4. Check the residues using prediction function for removing data noise.

```
SELECT items.*,
       madlib.linregr_predict(array[1,tax], m.coef) as
         predict, price -
           madlib.linregr_predict(array[1,tax], m.coef) as
             residual FROM items, items_lr quantity;
```

Refer `http://doc.madlib.net/v1.1/index.html` for more documentation on functions and examples.

Using Greenplum Chorus

Greenplum Chorus can integrate with the multidimensional data visualization tools from Tableau software. Chorus is capable of grabbing data from HDFS and Greenplum Databases and throws out the data into Tableau workbooks for advanced visualizations. It promotes real-time social collaboration and helps make projects more transparent.

It provides an integrated development environment for analytics. It can integrate with any third-party data and provide insights using visualization tools that can be third-party as well.

In Chorus, we have two sets to data types to work with:

- **Source dataset**: Supports both internal and external data with native connectivity to GPDB and flat files
- **Sandbox dataset**: Refers to the data generated as a result of running analytics

Chorus provides a single view GUI tool for exploring, aggregating, filtering, and moving data to the sandboxes.

Chorus integrates with Tableau workspace for advanced visual data analysis. The following screenshot demonstrates the usage of Tableau from Chorus GUI:

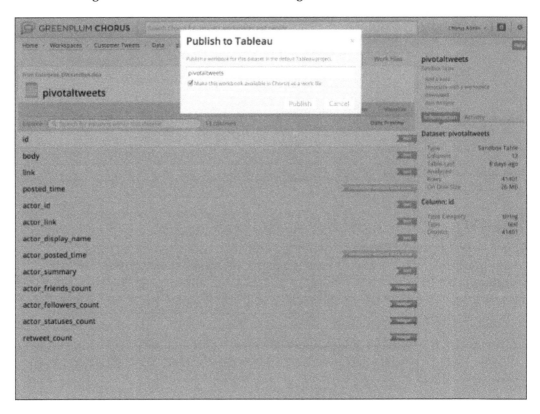

There is an open source version of Greenplum Chorus called OpenChorus. Refer `http://gopivotal.com/pivotal-products/pivotal-data-fabric/pivotal-chorus` for more details.

Pivotal

As mentioned in *Chapter 2, Greenplum Unified Analytics Platform (UAP)*, since April 2013, with the formation of Pivotal in collaboration with EMC and VMware, Greenplum UAP and data science product suite is being integrated with VMware's Spring Source products like Gemfire, and the products are being repositioned under the name of Pivotal. However, the current functions of the product will continue to exist. The following table shows the corresponding product names in Pivotal. Pivotal One product suite would now integrate.

Greenplum product names	Pivotal product names
Greenplum Database	Pivotal Greenplum Database
Greenplum DCA	Pivotal DCA
Greenplum UAP	Pivotal UAP
Greenplum HD	Pivotal HD
Greenplum Chorus	Pivotal Chorus
	Additionally, HAWQ framework for an integrated SQL-based querying between HD and GP DB. Also, In Memory Data Grid, Gemfire and SQLFire from the VMware suite are being integrated into Pivotal One solution.

References/Further reading

- Pivotal products: `http://www.gopivotal.com/pivotal-products`
- pgAdminIII Client: `http://www.pgadmin.org/docs/dev/index.html`
- Apache Pig tutorial: `http://pig.apache.org/docs/r0.7.0/tutorial.html`
- Apache Hive tutorial: `https://cwiki.apache.org/confluence/display/Hive/Tutorial`
- Sqoop User guide: `http://sqoop.apache.org/docs/1.4.0-incubating/SqoopUserGuide.html`
- MoreVRP for Greenplum: `http://morevrp.com/products/morevrp-for-pivotal-greenplum`

Summary

In this chapter, we have explored various implementation aspects of Greenplum UAP. We started with understanding data loading strategies for Greenplum and HD. We have looked at loading data into Greenplum using internal utilities and functions such as `gpload` and `gpfdist` and also using Informatica PowerExchange connector. For HD, we have explored Hive and Greenplum bulk loader utility.

We moved on to take a dive deep into distribution and partitioning aspects of Greenplum along with strategies for querying Greenplum and HD. We have looked at various functions such as `ANALYZE` and `EXPLAIN` to optimize the queries and interpretation of query plans. Finally, we have explored some in-database analytics options with Greenplum (using Windows function, integrating MADlib, and using PL/R). At the end of this chapter, readers should be fairly familiar with various implementation aspects of Greenplum in conjunction with Hadoop for implementing data storage and analytics for Big Data.

Index

Greenplum Database 29, 45, 46
HD 30, 52, 53
Compute layer 123
Confidence 74
configuration data 9
COPY command 95
CREATE FUNCTION command 134
CSV (Comma Separated Values) 50

D

data
  loading, techniques 20, 21
  setting up 20
  skewing 113
  sourcing, from Greenplum 109, 110
data analytics
  about 15, 16, 18
  drivers 16
  modeling methods 69
  paradigms 62
  techniques 18
data analytics, techniques 65
  classification 65, 66
  clustering 65, 67
  descriptive analytics 18
  forecasting 65-67
  optimization 65, 68
  prediction 65- 67
  predictive analytics 18
  regression 65-67
  simulations 65, 68
  specialized analytics 18
  usage 69
Data Computing Appliance. *See* **DCA**
data distribution
  about 52
  hash distribution 52
  round robin distribution 52
data exploration 20, 21
data formats, Big Data 13, 14
  semi-structured 13
  structured 13
  unstructured 14
Data Integration Accelerator. *See* **DIA**
Data Integration (DI) 16

data loading
  external tables, used 50
  patterns 41-45
data loading, patterns
  ELT 41
  ETL 41
  ETLT 42
data redundancy
  components, implementing 50
data science 19
data science life cycle
  about 19
  business problem, stating 19
  data exploration 20, 21
  data, setting up 20
  data transformation 20, 21
  effectiveness, measuring 22
  model, designing 21
  model, executing 21, 22
  publish insights 22
data streams 36
data transformation 20, 21
data warehouse
  about 32
  data, characteristics 32, 33
data warehousing 16, 32-35
Database layer 123
database modules 31
DBI Connector 136, 137
DCA
  about 26, 57, 58, 94, 123
  Compute layer 123
  Database layer 123
  DIA module 124
  Greenplum Database Compute module 124
  Greenplum Database Standard module 124
  HD Compute module 124
  HD module 124
  layer 123
  master server RAID configuration 125
  module 123
  monitoring 127-129
  Network layer 123
  segment server RAID configuration 126
  Storage layer 123
decision branch 71
decision node 71

M

MADlib
about 90
installing 90
URL 90
URL, for documentation 141
using, with Greenplum 139, 141
Mahout 30
massive parallel processing (MPP) systems
26, 38
master data 9
master host
about 46
functions 47
master node 105
functions 54
master server RAID configuration 125
mirror segment instance 50
model
designing 21, 22
executing 21, 22
modeling methods
about 69
association rules 69, 73-75
decision tree 69, 70, 72
K-means clustering 69, 80
linear regression 69, 77, 78
logistic regression 69, 78
Naive Bayesian classifier 69, 79, 80
text analysis 69, 81, 82
modules, UAP
about 31
database modules 31
DIA module 32
HD module 32
Multiple Instruction Single Data (MISD) 36
Multiple Instructions Multiple Data
(MIMD) 37

N

Naive Bayesian classifier 79, 80
Natural Language Processing (NLP) 16
Network layer 123
node
about 70
decision node 71

event node 71
terminal node 71
noisy data 12

O

ODBC drivers 49
OLAP database
about 34
vs, OLTP database 34
OLTP database
about 34
vs, OLAP database 34
OpenChorus
URL 142
operational data 15
optimization 68
ORDER BY clause 133
OVER clause 134

P

paradigms, data analytics 62
descriptive analytics 62, 63
predictive analytics 62-64
prescriptive analytics 62-65
parallel processing systems
about 36, 37
data streams 36
instruction streams 36
vs, distributed processing systems 36, 37
parsing 81
PARTITION BY clause 133
PDO 111, 42
Pentaho 106
Perl DBI 49
pgAdmin3 49
physical architecture, Greenplum Database
46-49
Pig 121, 122, 30
Pivotal 29, 142, 143
Pivotal Database 29
PL/R 137, 138
polymorphic data storage 51
PowerExchange connector. *See* **PWX**
connector
prediction 66, 67

U

UAP
  about 7, 25, 28
  architecture 32
  components 29, 45
  modules 31
Unified Analytics Platform (UAP)
unstructured data
  about 14
  characteristics 14
unsupervised analysis 65
unsupported data types, Greenplum 110
user-defined aggregates 135, 136

V

Vector 85

W

**Waikato Environment for Knowledge
    Analysis (Weka)**
Weka
  about 87-89
  features 87
  URL 87
  using, with Greenplum 138

window function
  about 132, 133
  characteristics 132
  creating 134
  dropping 134
  modifying 134
  ORDER BY clause 133
  OVER clause 134
  PARTITION BY clause 133
writable external tables 51, 98

Y

YARN 30

Z

ZooKeeper 30

Thank you for buying
Getting Started with Greenplum for Big Data Analytics

About Packt Publishing

Packt, pronounced 'packed', published its first book "Mastering phpMyAdmin for Effective MySQL Management" in April 2004 and subsequently continued to specialize in publishing highly focused books on specific technologies and solutions.

Our books and publications share the experiences of your fellow IT professionals in adapting and customizing today's systems, applications, and frameworks. Our solution based books give you the knowledge and power to customize the software and technologies you're using to get the job done. Packt books are more specific and less general than the IT books you have seen in the past. Our unique business model allows us to bring you more focused information, giving you more of what you need to know, and less of what you don't.

Packt is a modern, yet unique publishing company, which focuses on producing quality, cutting-edge books for communities of developers, administrators, and newbies alike. For more information, please visit our website: www.packtpub.com.

About Packt Enterprise

In 2010, Packt launched two new brands, Packt Enterprise and Packt Open Source, in order to continue its focus on specialization. This book is part of the Packt Enterprise brand, home to books published on enterprise software – software created by major vendors, including (but not limited to) IBM, Microsoft and Oracle, often for use in other corporations. Its titles will offer information relevant to a range of users of this software, including administrators, developers, architects, and end users.

Writing for Packt

We welcome all inquiries from people who are interested in authoring. Book proposals should be sent to author@packtpub.com. If your book idea is still at an early stage and you would like to discuss it first before writing a formal book proposal, contact us; one of our commissioning editors will get in touch with you.

We're not just looking for published authors; if you have strong technical skills but no writing experience, our experienced editors can help you develop a writing career, or simply get some additional reward for your expertise.

Hadoop Real-World Solutions Cookbook

ISBN: 978-1-84951-912-0   Paperback: 316 pages

Realistic, simple code examples to aolve problems at scale with Hadoop and related technologies

1. Solutions to common problems when working in the Hadoop environment

2. Recipes for (un)loading data, analytics, and troubleshooting

3. In depth code examples demonstrating various analytic models, analytic solutions, and common best practices

Microsoft SQL Server 2012 with Hadoop

ISBN: 978-1-78217-798-2   Paperback: 96 pages

Integrate data between Apache Hadoop and SQL Server 2012 and prove business intelligence on the heterogeneous data

1. Integrate data from unstructured (Hadoop) and structured (SQL Server 2012) sources

2. Configure and install connectors for a bi-directional transfer of data

3. Full of illustrations, diagrams, and tips with clear, step-by-step instructions and practical examples

Please check **www.PacktPub.com** for information on our titles

Implementing Splunk: Big Data Reporting and Development for Operational Intelligence

ISBN: 978-1-84969-328-8   Paperback: 448 pages

Learn to transform your machine data into valuable IT and business insights with this comprehensive and practical tutorial

1. Learn to search, dashboard, configure, and deploy Splunk on one machine or thousands

2. Start working with Splunk fast, with a tested set of practical examples and useful advice

3. Step-by-step instructions and examples with a comprehensive coverage for Splunk veterans and newbies alike.

Scaling Big Data with Hadoop and Solr

ISBN:978-1-78328-137-4   Paperback: 144 pages

Learn exciting new ways to build efficient, high performance enterprise search repositories for Big Data using Hadoop and Solr

1. Understand the different approaches of making Solr work on Big Data as well as the benefits and drawbacks

2. Learn from interesting, real-life use cases for Big Data search along with sample code

3. Work with the Distributed Enterprise Search without prior knowledge of Hadoop and Solr

Please check **www.PacktPub.com** for information on our titles